MW00379912

BEAVIS AND BUTT-HEAD
DO AMERICA

THE OFFICIAL SCRIPT BOOK

WRITTEN BY: MIKE JUDGE/JOE STILLMAN

books
MTV BOOKS/POCKET BOOKS

Beavis and Butt-head are not role models. They're not even human.
They're cartoons. Some of the things they do would cause a
real person to get hurt, expelled, arrested, possibly deported.
To put it another way: Don't try this at home.

Beavis and Butt-head
Created by Mike Judge

Written by: Mike Judge/Joe Stillman

Script Consultants: Kristofor Brown/Larry Doyle

Storyboard Artists: Ilya Skorupsky, Chris Prynosky, Mike DeSeve, Brian Mulroney, Kevin Brownie,
Mike Labash, Ted Stern, Ray DaSilva, Guy Moore

Color Images: Michael A. Baez, Koari Hamura, Sophie Kitteredge, Bill Long, Brian Moyer, Bill Schwab,
Monica Smith, Freya Tanz

Flip Animation: Brad MacDonald, Bryon Moore, Rich Kranz

Cover: Paramount Pictures/MTV Networks

Special thanks at MTV to: John Andrews, Christine Brown, Kris Brown, Cindy Charles, Sara Duffy,
Sharon Fitzgerald, David Gale, Andrea LaBate, Lucia Ludovico, Dominie Mahl, Renee Presser, Lisa
Silfen, Robin Silverman, Donald Silvey, Abby Terkuhle, Van Toffler, and James D Wood.

Special thanks at Pocket Books to: Lynda Castillo, Gina Centrello, Felice Javit,
Liate Stehlik, Dave Stern, Kara Welsh, and Irene Yuss.

"Fly High, Lesbian Seagull," words and music by Tom Wilson Weinberg.
Published by Above Ground Music (ASCAP). All Rights Reserved. Reprinted with Permission.

An Original Publication of MTV Books/Pocket Books

POCKET BOOKS, a division of Simon and Schuster, Inc.
1230 Avenue of the Americas, New York NY 10020

This book is a work of fiction. Names, characters, places, and incidents are either products
of the author's imagination or are used fictitiously.

Copyright © 1996 by MTV Networks, a division of Viacom International, Inc.

All rights reserved, including the right to reproduce this book or portions thereof in any form
whatsoever. For information address Pocket Books, 1230 Avenue of the Americas, New York NY 10020

ISBN: 0-671-00658-4

First MTV Books/Pocket Books trade paperback printing January 1997

10 9 8 7 6 5 4 3 2 1

Pocket and colophon are registered trademarks of Simon and Schuster Inc.

MTV: MUSIC TELEVISION, Beavis and Butt-head Do America and all related titles, logos and characters
are trademarks of MTV Networks, a division of Viacom International Inc.

Printed in the U.S.A.

The sale of this book without its cover is unauthorized.
If you purchased this book without a cover, you should be
aware that it was reported to the publisher as "unsold
and destroyed." Neither the author nor the publisher has
received payment for the sale of this "stripped book."

<u>FOREWORD</u>

By Mike Judge

I'm not quite sure what to write in this here "Foreword."

I usually skip the foreword when I read a book, and come to think of it,

I don't think I've ever seen a screenplay with a foreword in it.

I figure if you have this screenplay, you are either a really big *Beavis*

and Butt-head fan or a person who hates *Beavis and Butt-head* and someone

bought this for you as a joke-present. In the latter case, you probably

won't ever read this anyway, so I guess I'm addressing the fans here and

maybe I'll just give you a brief history of the movie.

The *Beavis and Butt-head* TV series first aired on Monday, March

8th of 1993. Saturday of that week or the next week (I don't quite

remember), there was an article about the show on the cover of the

entertainment section of the *LA Times*. The following Monday almost

every movie studio in Hollywood was calling, wanting to make a movie.

I don't think any of them had actually even watched the show. They just

read the article and saw it as another knockoff of *Wayne's World* or *Bill*

and Ted. As I recall, every studio except for one, wanted to do the

movie live-action. I love live-action movies and I'd like to do one

some day, but I just didn't see how *Beavis and Butt-head* could work as a

live-action movie. I wish it could have, because animation is

a huge pain in the ass.

So, I went out to Hollywood and met with all kinds of movie
executives. I should have been more excited about it than I was, but it
all just seemed really weird. I mean, the show had only been on the air
for two weeks and all of a sudden everyone wanted to make a movie. And
half of these people had hardly even seen the show. I could tell some
of them didn't even like it. (I couldn't blame them either. The first
couple shows were pretty bad I thought. It wasn't until the show went
on the air again in May that the good episodes started coming out.)

That summer, it looked like the movie was really going to happen.
Then some kind of dispute happened over which studio had the rights.
I won't go into it here. It's all pretty dull and you can read about it
in back issues of *The Wall Street Journal,* but basically it stalled the
movie for about two years.

Sometime in the summer of '95 everything was finally settled.
The movie was to be done with Paramount, Geffen Pictures, and MTV Films.
That's right folks, three big movie companies. I'm a lucky guy.

I wanted to get the same thirty-two writers who wrote the
Flintstones movie to write this, but a couple of them weren't available.
I said, "If I can't get all thirty-two, I don't want any of 'em."
You just don't mess with chemistry like that. So, I decided to write
the screenplay myself with Joe Stillman, a writer who has done
a lot of writing for the show.

I think this has been the fastest an animated feature

has ever been made. I started recording my voices for the beginning

of the movie while I was still finishing writing the ending.

What you have here is the version of the script that we started

recording voices and storyboarding from (minus some small changes made

by our legal department). It's a little different from what the movie

ended up being, because there's always a lot of improvising and a lot

that changes as the animation process starts. There have also been

several lines and scenes cut.

You might notice that sometimes the humor of *Beavis and Butt-head*

doesn't always work when it's written on a page. Luckily for me, this

thing started out as an animated short I made in the privacy of my own

home. I think I would have had a hell of a time trying to get someone

to produce a script that was full of lines like, "Huh huh huh. Anus.

Huh huh huh."

Enjoy,

Mike Judge.

ABBREVIATIONS

EXT.   EXTERIOR
INT.   INTERIOR
                        Used to help establish the setting of a scene

EST.   ESTABLISHING SHOT - a shot used to establish setting

O.C. or O.S.   OFF CAMERA/OFF SCREEN - the character is not
                        seen in the shot

V.O.   VOICE OVER - the character's voice is heard,
                        but he/she is not seen

P.O.V.   POINT OF VIEW - shows the action from the
                        perspective of the indicated character
                        or characters

CONT.   CONTINUED - same character continues speaking

SFX   SOUND EFFECTS

The movie begins with scenes of people screaming in horror and running down the streets of a big city. The ground shakes from what seems like giant foot steps. There are pieces of building debris falling everywhere, people getting crushed, power lines coming down, etc. — complete pandemonium. It all looks very much like a Japanese animated King-Kong or Godzilla movie. We hear the footsteps getting closer and the ground shaking becomes more intense - more debris falling. Then we see a HUGE BLACK TENNIS SHOE come into frame and smash a National Guard truck. As we pan up, we see the white socks, then the red shorts, the AC/DC T-shirt, then we hear the familiar, "Huh huh huh." - only it's a huge sound...this is a THREE-HUNDRED FOOT TALL BUTT-HEAD. "Butt-Kong" continues his path of destruction - stomping on cars and buildings and saying, "This is cool. Huh huh huh."

Airplanes and tanks start firing at Butt-Head (Butt-Kong). He looks irritated and says, "Cut it out butt-munch!" Butt-Head swats at the planes, sending them crashing to the ground and stomps on the tanks. Then, something catches his eye. Butt-Head reaches into a skyscraper and picks up a nice looking woman — a lot like the one from the King Kong movie. He looks down at her in his hand and goes wide-eyed, "Whoa! Huh huh huh." The woman screams in terror as Butt-Head looks down at her and tries a few lame pick up lines. "Uuuh...Hey baby. I'm like, pretty tall. Huh huh huh." He swats down a helicopter that is circling his head, "Dammit, I'm trying to score!" The helicopter goes down in flames. We CUT TO some guys sitting on a tank firing at him. They notice giant footsteps coming from the other direction and turn the tank around. Through their binoculars we see a THREE-HUNDRED FOOT BEAVIS coming from the horizon. The giant Beavis is even more destructive than Butt-Kong (maybe he could be breathing fire). Beavis starts trying to pick up on Butt-Head's woman. Butt-Head puts the woman down and he and Beavis begin to go at it, leveling the city with one of their stupid juvenile smack-fights.

We CROSS-DISSOLVE from three-hundred foot Beavis shaking Butt-Kong to Butt-Head asleep on the couch with Beavis shaking him.

INT.   B&B'S HOME - DAY

                    BEAVIS (O.C.)
          Butt-Head! Butt-Head! Hey, Butt-Head!

Butt-Head is dead asleep on the couch. Beavis shakes him.

                    BEAVIS
          Butt-Head, wake up, wake up!

Butt-Head comes around.

                    BUTT-HEAD
          Dammit, Beavis, I was about to score. Huh
          huh.

                    BEAVIS
          Yeah, but check it out. It's gone!

BUTT-HEAD
What's gone?

BEAVIS
The TV.

Beavis is making STRANGE NOISES, in a state of shock.

Butt-Head rubs his eyes and looks at the empty space where the TV was.

BUTT-HEAD
Uuuuuuh, huh huh. Uuh,...

Out the window, we see two YOUNG MEN carrying B&B's TV into their van.

Still on the couch, Butt-Head looks over at the broken window. We see a
CROW BAR lying on the floor, and the front door left open.

Butt-Head looks at the BROKEN WINDOW, at the CROWBAR, the OPEN DOOR,
then back at the EMPTY SPACE where the TV was. He does this a couple of
times — piecing it all together.

BUTT-HEAD (CONT.)
Whoa! I think I just figured something out
Beavis.

BEAVIS
What?

BUTT-HEAD
This sucks.

BEAVIS
Yeah, heh heh.

Beavis is still in shock. They both stare at the empty space where the
TV was for a beat, not quite sure what to do.

Beavis is SHAKING AND MAKING WEIRD NOISES. He presses buttons on the
remote a few times, as if it might help somehow.

BUTT-HEAD
This sucks more than anything that has
ever sucked before. We must find this
butt-hole that took the TV.

2

EXT.   CITY STREET - NIGHT

Bad neighborhood. 70's music blares.

A fast driving car drives right at us and stops. Punks run in fear.
Beavis hops out of the driver's seat, wearing bell bottoms, chain
jewelry and a 70's afro. Into a dramatic CLOSE-UP, he takes off his
glasses.

FREEZE ON BEAVIS

                    ANNOUNCER
          Beavis!

FRAME UNFREEZES. Beavis whips out a huge gun.

                    BEAVIS
          Freeze, butt-wipe!

An attacker comes from one side. Beavis uses Judo. Another tosses a
knife. Beavis ducks, then shoots with two hands, police style.

INT.   BEDROOM - NIGHT

Swinger's pad. Totally 70's. A group of bikini'd girls on a waterbed.
Butt-Head approaches them. He wears a leisure suit, collar way open. He
plops down in the bed.

FREEZE ON BUTT-HEAD

                    ANNOUNCER
          Butt-Head!

FRAME UNFREEZES. The girls wrap their arms around him.

                    BUTT-HEAD
          Huh huh huh. Come to Butt-Head, Baby.

                    ANNOUNCER
          Star in...

MAIN TITLE - FULL FRAME

EXT. CITY STREETS - DAY/NIGHT

ACTION MONTAGE BEGINS. Styled like a 70's cop show opening.

OPENING CREDITS to the movie appear just as cop show credits would.

Beavis does a Starsky and Hutch-style roll with a gun.

Butt-Head slaps a pimp.

3

Beavis drives, chasing a car.

Butt-Head is slapped by a girl.

                    BUTT-HEAD
          Huh huh huh. That was cool.

Beavis and Butt-Head are in a warehouse shoot-out.

A black police chief rises from a desk to yell at B&B.

B&B dive for cover just before a building explodes.

In CLOSE UP, Beavis smiles for an ID shot.

Butt-Head does the same.

Beavis, in a rooftop fight, kicks his opponent over the edge.

A beautiful woman, back to us, takes off her dress for Butt-Head. FINAL
OPENING CREDIT APPEARS. Butt-Head and the woman fall into bed.
Suddenly...

INT. SCHOOL HALLWAY/DOOR TO A.V. ROOM - DAY

From inside, SOUND of equipment crashing.

B&B come out wheeling a TV on one of those carts. There are cables
attached to it still leading back into the A.V. room. As they push the
cart we hear more equipment falling.

                    BUTT-HEAD
          Dammit, it's stuck.

They give it one big push and it finally breaks free. We see that the
cables are tangled with cables from other TVs and VCRs, which all come
crashing to the ground.

                 BUTT-HEAD (CONT.)
          Huh huh huh. That was cool.

                      BEAVIS
          Yeah, heh heh. Let's just wheel this thing
          back to the house.

INT. SCHOOL/ANOTHER HALLWAY - DAY

MR. VAN DRIESSEN stops B&B.

                   VAN DRIESSEN
          Ah, excuse me boys. What's going on here?

4

BUTT-HEAD

Uh, someone stole our TV.

BEAVIS

Yeah. We're just gonna use this one. Get outta the way. Heh heh.

VAN DRIESSEN

I'm afraid that TV belongs to the school. Mmmkay? You know, this could be a positive experience for you guys. There's a wonderful world out there when we discover we don't need TV to entertain us.

BUTT-HEAD

Huh huh huh. He said "anus."

BEAVIS
(to himself)
Entert-ain...us...an-us..Oh yeah! Heh heh. Anus. Heh heh.

VAN DRIESSEN
(frustrated)
Have you guys heard a word I've said?

BUTT-HEAD

Yeah, "anus". Huh huh huh huh.

VAN DRIESSEN

Look guys, just take the TV back to the A.V. room right now. And try to be a little more open-minded. Mmkay?

Van Driessen leaves. B&B continue to wheel the cart home.

BUTT-HEAD

What a dork. Huh huh.

BEAVIS

Yeah, heh heh. He's a anus. Heh heh.

EXT. SCHOOL/STAIRWAY - DAY

B&B arrive with the cart at the top of a stairway. They lamely attempt to let it slowly down the steps. The cart is too top-heavy and goes tumbling to the bottom of the stairs, shattering the TV.

BUTT-HEAD

Huh huh huh. That was cool.

BEAVIS

No it wasn't!

5

BUTT-HEAD
Uh,...Oh yeah.

B&B stand at the top of the stairs looking down at the wreckage.
PRINCIPAL McVICKER shows up by the TV.

McVICKER
Why.... You... You bastards... Ge... get
out! You're suspended. One more screw
up... and you're expelled.

B&B walk off laughing.

EXT.   THE ANDERSON'S DRIVEWAY - DUSK

B&B walk up. There's a camper in the driveway.

BUTT-HEAD
Whoa, check it out Beavis. I didn't know
Anderson had a Camper.

BEAVIS
Yeah, heh heh. Maybe it has a TV. Heh heh.
TV.

B&B walk up to the camper and start to open the door just as MARCY
ANDERSON opens it. (as usual, she doesn't recognize them.)

MARCY
Oh, hello. Are you guys here to look at
the refrigerator?

BUTT-HEAD
Uh, no.

BEAVIS
We're here to look at the TV. Heh heh.

MARCY
Oh, I didn't realize it was broken. Come
on in.

BUTT-HEAD
Cool. Huh huh huh.

B&B walk into the camper. Marcy stays outside.

6

EXT. ANDERSON'S CAMPER - SAME TIME

Tom is adjusting the trailer-hitch. Marcy watches.

> **TOM**
> Well that oughtta hold her. Ya know, the
> most important thing you can have on a
> camper is a good propane regulator, and
> this here's the best one they make.

> **MARCY**
> I sure hope we can get the 'fridge fixed
> before we leave.

> **TOM**
> Now Marcy, we've been savin' for this trip
> our whole lives and we're gonna go come
> Hell or high water...

Through the camper walls, we hear the faint sound of B&B AIR/MOUTH-
GUITARING "IRON MAN."

> **TOM** (CONT.)
> What the hell is that noise?

INT. ANDERSON'S CAMPER - DUSK.

B&B watch a "Cops"-type show. Beavis gets up, goes to the refrigerator
and grabs a soda. The refrigerator is under the counter on which the TV
is sitting.

Beavis takes a sip and then does a SPIT TAKE, SPRAYING SODA ALL OVER THE
TOP OF THE TV.

> **BEAVIS**
> AAAAAAGH!!! This crap is warm!

ANGLE ON TV: The soda Beavis spit out drips into the inside of the TV.
We see smoke and hear SIZZLING AND SHORT CIRCUIT SFX. The TV goes dead.

> **BUTT-HEAD**
> Beavis, you butt-hole! You broke it.

EXT. ANDERSON'S CAMPER - DAY

B&B come out. Tom notices them.

> **TOM**
> Hey, what's goin' on here?

> **MARCY**
> They're here to fix the TV, Tom.

7

                         TOM
          The TV ain't broken.

                      BUTT-HEAD
          Yeah it is. Huh huh huh.

Tom adjust his glasses as he looks at B&B.

TOM'S BLURRY P.O.V.: We see B&B out of focus.

                         TOM
          Hey wait a minute. You two look kinda
          familiar. Ain't you them kids that've been
          whackin' off in my tool shed?

                  BEAVIS & BUTT-HEAD
          Huh huh huh huh huh.

ANGLE ON BEAVIS: looking particularly guilty, eyes shifting back and
forth.

B&B walk off, leaving Tom wondering.

EXT. STREET IN A SEEDY PART OF TOWN - JUST BEFORE DAWN.

B&B are having TV withdrawal. Butt-Head is bug-eyed. Beavis has the
shakes bad, arms folded like Dustin Hoffman in "Midnight Cowboy".

                       BEAVIS
          Nnnnooo. Oooooh nooooo.

                      BUTT-HEAD
          What's your problem Beavis?

                       BEAVIS
          I need TV now! Now! NNNNDAMMIT!!!

Butt-Head stops short. He looks up. His face is bathed in a golden,
throbbing light.

BUTT-HEAD'S P.O.V.:   We see a flashing neon sign that says, "TV".
Pull back to show B&B are standing outside the Elite Motel Lodge,
featuring "Color TV" and "Air-Cooled Rooms", with "Special Nap Rates".

B&B stare up, as if at a god.

                       BEAVIS
                     (crazed)
          Heh heh. TV. Heh Teee Veee.

EXT. MOTEL COURT - CONTINUOUS

Butt-Head tries the first door. It's locked. He tries the second door. It's locked. He tries the third door. It opens.

B&B's eyes bulge. Inside, PRINCIPAL McVICKER is lying across the legs of an obvious prostitute, his pants pulled down. She SPANKS him.

                    McVICKER
          Please mmm... may I have another?!

B&B LAUGH. McVicker hears and looks up.

                    McVICKER (Cont.)
          Beavis and Butt-Head! y...y...you
          bastards.

                    BEAVIS
          Can we watch your TV?

                    McVICKER
          Y... Y... You're expelled! Get out!

Butt-Head closes the door, laughing, and starts to walk towards the next door. The muffled sound of a SPANK can be heard followed by McVicker asking for another.

                    BUTT-HEAD
          Huh huh huh. That was cool.

                    BEAVIS
          Dammit! I need a TV now! We're missing
          everything!

INT. MOTEL ROOM - CONTINUOUS

The only light in the room is a flickering TV. Sitting on the bed, talking on the phone is MUDDY. He's a tough, mean looking red-neck — a Jack Ruby type.

On the nightstand next to him is a three-quarter drunk bottle of bourbon and a manila envelope. On his lap, is a big gun.

                    MUDDY
          ...Are you sure these guys can pull this
          off? It's gotta look like an accident...

We hear a knock on the door and muffled B&B laughs.

                    MUDDY (CONT.)
          Hold on a minute. That must be them now.
          I'll call you back. (Hangs up
          phone)...Come in!

9

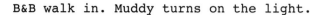

B&B walk in. Muddy turns on the light.

>   **BEAVIS**
>   (sounding suddenly sedated)
>   Aaaah. TeeeVeeeee, heh heh.

>   **MUDDY**
>   Yer late.

>   **BUTT-HEAD**
>   Why? Did we miss American Gladiators?

MUDDY'S P.O.V.: B&B are a drunken blur.

>   **MUDDY**
>   Well, Earl said you guys were young, but
>   jeez... Oh well, as long as you can get
>   the job done. So what are your names?

>   **BUTT-HEAD**
>   Uh, Butt-Head.

>   **BEAVIS**
>   Beavis.

>   **MUDDY**
>   That's alright. I'd rather not know your
>   real names anyways. I'm Muddy. Look, I'm
>   gonna get right to the point. I'll pay you
>   ten grand plus expenses, all payable after
>   you do her...

>   **BUTT-HEAD**
>   (full of innuendo)
>   Do her? Huh huh.

>   **MUDDY**
>   That's right. I'm offering you ten grand
>   plus expenses to do my wife. We gotta
>   deal?

Butt-Head stares in shock.

>   **BEAVIS**
>   Actually, we just wanna watch TV...

>   **BUTT-HEAD**
>   Shut up Beavis! Uh, Yeah. We'll do your
>   wife.

>   **BEAVIS**
>   (trembling)
>   Nnnnaah...We need to watch TV DAMMIT!!!

Butt-Head SMACKS Beavis and pulls him aside.

>   **BUTT-HEAD**
>   Beavis, you butt-munch, this guy wants us
>   to score with his wife. And he's gonna pay
>   us. We can buy a new TV.

>   **BEAVIS**
>   Oh, heh heh really? Cool. Heh heh.

>   **BUTT-HEAD**
>   (to Muddy)
>   Uh, huh huh... We'll do it, sir.

>   **MUDDY**
>   Okay, then let's get down to business.

ANGLE ON THE BED. Muddy slaps down a picture of DALLAS, his wife.
Leather clad, biker, beautiful.

>   **MUDDY** (CONT.)
>   Here she is. Her name's Dallas. She ain't
>   as sweet as she looks. She stole
>   everything from me. Ya gotta watch out,
>   'cause she'll do you twice as fast as
>   you'd do her.

>   **BUTT-HEAD**
>   Whoa, huh huh. Cool.

Muddy plunks down PLANE TICKETS.

>   **MUDDY**
>   She's holed up in a hotel room in Las
>   Vegas. Your flight leaves in a couple of
>   hours. Now c'mon, I'll drive you to the
>   airport.

>   **BUTT-HEAD**
>   Holed up. Huh huh huh. Holed.

>   **BEAVIS**
>   Can we watch some TV first?

Muddy picks up the gun and SHOOTS the TV.

>   **MUDDY**
>   No.

EXT. CITY STREETS - MORNING

Muddy driving his loud four-by-four like a maniac, drunk with bloodshot
eyes. B&B are in the back seat. He eyes them through the rearview.
Meanwhile, a cat bounces off the windshield with a SHRIEK.

>   **MUDDY**
>   One more thing. Mah wife's got this
>   leather satchel. It's black about this
>   big. I need ya to bring it back. It's real
>   important. Sentimental value... Any
>   questions so far?

>   **BUTT-HEAD**
>   Uh, yeah. Does she have big hooters?

>   **MUDDY**
>   She sure does.

>   **BUTT-HEAD**
>   This is gonna be Cool! Huh huh huh.

>   **BEAVIS**
>   Yeah, heh heh. Boooooiiiing!!!

>   **MUDDY**
>   Just make sure it looks like an
>   accident...

>   **BEAVIS**
>   (spastic)
>   Yeah, heh heh. I think <u>I</u> just had an
>   accident. Heh heh hmm heh hmm heh.

>   **MUDDY**
>   Huh huh. You guys are funny. Let's have a
>   drink on it.

Muddy swigs the last swallow from his bottle of bourbon.

EXT. AIRPORT - EARLY MORNING

In an overhead view, the four-by-four screeches up to the gate,
fishtails to a stop, throwing B&B on to the sidewalk, and peels away.

>   **BUTT-HEAD**
>   We're gonna get paid to score.

>   **BEAVIS**
>   Yeah, heh heh, and then we're gonna get a
>   big-screen TV! Heh heh.

> **BUTT-HEAD**
> Beavis, this is the greatest day of our
> lives. Huh huh huh.

INT.   AIRPLANE - DAY

B&B enter the plane. They sit down in the first two seats on the right —
in First Class. A flight attendant, DOLORIS approaches them.

> **DOLORIS**
> Hi. Can I help you find your seats?

> **BUTT-HEAD**
> Uuh, nah. These seats are OK.

> **DOLORIS**
> I think your tickets have you guys seated
> in row fourteen, coach. So why don't you
> just go ahead and move back OK?

> **BUTT-HEAD**
> That's OK. Someone else can have those.

> **BEAVIS**
> Yeah, it's not that important to me,
> really. Those seats are too small anyways.

Doloris yanks them out of their seats and leads them down the aisle.

ANGLE DOWN AISLE in coach. Doloris stops by a row where an elderly
woman, MARTHA, sits by the window. Next to her: Two empty seats.

> **DOLORIS**
> Here you are.

She gestures to the seats and leaves. Beavis climbs in the middle, Butt-
Head in the aisle - still watching Doloris.

> **BUTT-HEAD**
> Hey Beavis. When she was leading us down
> here, huh huh, she touched my butt. Huh
> huh huh.

Martha, her senses a bit dimmed from age, turns to B&B.

> **MARTHA**
> Hello there. Are you two heading for Las
> Vegas?

> **BEAVIS**
> Yeah, we're gonna score.

13

MARTHA
I hope to score big there myself. I'm
mostly going to be doing the slots.

BEAVIS
Yeah, I'm hoping to do some sluts too. Heh
heh. Do they have lots of sluts in Las
Vegas?

MARTHA
Oh, there are so many slots you won't know
where to begin.

BEAVIS
Whoa! Heh heh. Hey Butt-Head, this chick
is pretty cool. She says there's gonna be
tons of sluts in Las Vegas! Heh heh heh.

BUTT-HEAD
Cool. Huh huh huh.

MARTHA
It's so nice to meet young men who are so
well mannered.

BEAVIS
Yeah, heh heh. I'm gonna have money, and a
big screen TV and sluts everywhere!

MARTHA
Oh, that's nice.

CAPTAIN'S VOICE (V.O.)
(through P.A.)
Good morning. This is your captain
speaking. Welcome aboard flight 151
non-stop to Las Vegas. We ask that you
turn your attention to the front of
the cabin for pre-flight safety
instructions.

B&B see Doloris, stepping nearby to demonstrate the seat belt.

ATTENDANT'S VOICE
To fasten your seat belt, insert the free
end into the coupling.

BUTT-HEAD
Insert. Huh huh huh.

Doloris demonstrates. B&B are dumbfounded. It's too complicated.

BUTT-HEAD (CONT.)
Uh....

14

They struggle to make their seat belts fit, getting each other's parts.

                    TAMMY (O.C.)
          Hi, I'm Tammy. Can I help you with that?

Butt-Head looks up.

From his P.O.V. we see a beautiful woman, TAMMY, smiling, her hands reaching down. FALLING IN LOVE/HARP MUSIC STING plays.

CLOSE on Butt-Head's lap as two female hands reach down and pull one strap from between Butt-Head's legs.

Butt-Head looks down at his lap as Tammy leans over him. A loud CLICKING can be heard. Butt-Head stares blankly.

                    TAMMY (CONT.)
          There you go. You're all set.

                    BUTT-HEAD
               (stunned)
          I love you.

Suddenly Martha buckles Beavis' belt. Tammy goes.

                    BEAVIS
          Wait, I wanted her to do it.

                    BUTT-HEAD
          Huh huh. Soon, she will be mine.

                    CAPTAIN'S VOICE
          Flight attendants, please prepare for
          take-off.

The engines start to hum. The plane is rolling.

Butt-Head struggles to get his seat belt off. He does everything but pull the handle. Beavis goes white with fear.

The plane starts to shake. The engines rumble. Beavis starts to freak.

                    BEAVIS
          Hey wait a minute. What's going on?!

Butt-Head bangs away at his seat belt. Beavis looks out the window and realizes they're in the air.

                    BEAVIS (CONT.)
               (screams)
          Aaaagh!!! We're gonna die!!!!!

ANGLE ON COUPLE IN FRONT OF B&B:

> **MAN**
> D'ya hear that? Something must be wrong!

> **WOMAN**
> Oh my God!!!!!!!

ANGLE ON CABIN, people start screaming. The plane quakes, lifting up.

ON BUTT-HEAD, furiously pulling:

> **BUTT-HEAD**
> Dammit! Huh huh. That chick wants me.

> **BEAVIS**
> Aggghg! We're gonna die! We're all gonna
> die!

The plane arcs upwards. Butt-Head finally gets the belt off as the plane is in full thrust. He rises and goes tumbling backward down the aisle.

ON PEOPLE seeing Butt-Head flying, screaming in panic.

In free fall:

Butt-Head grabs the door to the hangable luggage. It all comes tearing out.

Butt-Head flies up, hitting several overhead luggage racks, which open and spill their contents.

Butt-Head lands in the galley, causing food to go flying and coffee to pour freely.

ON THE CABIN as the plane starts to level out. People stop their screaming.

ON BUTT-HEAD, underneath the rubble, poking his head out. He's directly across from the flight attendant station where Tammy is strapped in.

> **BUTT-HEAD**
> Uh, huh huh... could you, like, do that
> thing with my belt again?

INT.   PLANE - LATER

All's in order. Flight attendants roll the beverage cart up the aisle. People read, relaxed.

ON BEAVIS AND MARTHA. Martha is showing pictures of her grandchildren. Beavis is showing the picture of Dallas that Muddy gave him.

                    BEAVIS
          I'm probably going to make out with her
          first before we, you know, get down...

                    MARTHA
          You'll have to speak up son. I have this
          ringing in my ears. My doctor says it
          could be related to my heart palpitations.
          I've had two operations on my heart.

                    BEAVIS
          Really? I poop too much.

                    MARTHA
          Oh, maybe you're lactose intolerant.

                    BEAVIS
          Uh... No, (louder) I poop too much. Then I
          get tired.

                    MARTHA
          Well, if you find yourself getting tired,
          take a couple of these.

She hands him a box of NoDrowz.

                    MARTHA (CONT.)
          They perk me right up.

                    BEAVIS
          Heh heh, thanks.

He pours the contents in his hand and chews them like candy. Then his
eyes open wide.

                    BEAVIS (CONT.)
                    (strange)
          Uh, tastes like crap. Heh heh. Mmmmm.

Beavis starts wolfing them down.

INT.   PLANE - A BIT LATER

Tammy passes out meals from a rolling cart. She works with Doloris.
Butt-Head stands behind Tammy, attempting to hit on her.

                    BUTT-HEAD
                    (to Tammy)
          So, uh huh huh, are you going to Las
          Vegas? Huh huh huh.

Tammy ignores him and moves on, leaving Butt-Head there.

ANGLE ON BUTT-HEAD, looking down at something.

PAN DOWN to reveal he's looking at a BEER on a fat guy's tray. The guy's asleep.

Butt-Head picks up the beer.

ANGLE ON BEAVIS, nearby. The NoDrowz is starting to take effect. Beavis starts shaking, babbling, staring cross-eyed at his fist, etc. (pre-Cornholio stuff)

Tammy reaches her next passenger.

>   **TAMMY**
>   Hi, we're serving dinner. Our selections
>   tonight are chicken piccata or seafood
>   gumbo...

>   **BEAVIS** (O.S.)
>   Piccata? Piccata! Picattatta tatta!

Tammy moves forward, leaving Butt-Head standing there. In the background, we see Beavis starting to quake, on the verge of Cornholio mode.

>   **PASSENGER**
>   Does the gumbo have corn in it?

ANGLE ON BEAVIS: Turned, facing the cabin, T-shirt pulled over his head in full Cornholio mode.

>   **BEAVIS**
>   I am Cornholio! I need piccata for my
>   bunghole!

>   **TAMMY**
>   You'll have to wait your turn sir.

>   **BEAVIS**
>   Are you threatening me? My bunghole will
>   not wait!

Beavis starts to wander down the aisle.

ANGLE ON CURTAIN TO FIRST CLASS CABIN. Beavis enters. From the other side, SOUND of screams. We hear several CALL BUTTONS being pressed.

ON BUTT-HEAD. He approaches Tammy from behind. She ignores him.

>   **BUTT-HEAD**
>   Uh, I got a beer. Want some? Huh huh.

ANGLE INSIDE THE COCKPIT.

The PILOTS are relaxed and settled in when the door to the cockpit slams open. Beavis is in the doorway SCREAMING.

                    BEAVIS
          Bargarajjjaaaahhh!!! I am Cornholio!!

The pilots SCREAM. The copilot jumps up so fast he causes coffee to spill everywhere, including on the captain's lap. The captain then jumps up, hitting the controls and SENDING THE PLANE INTO A NOSE-DIVE.

ON BUTT-HEAD

In the back of the plane standing next to Tammy. He starts to take a sip of beer. The nose-dive of the plane causes Butt-Head to go FLYING TOWARDS THE FRONT OF THE PLANE.

                    BUTT-HEAD
          AAAAAHHH!!! Huh huh. AAAAHHH!!!

Butt-Head bounces all over the plane and then gets tangled up in the curtain that separates first class and coach. It tears off, and he continues to fly forward.

COCKPIT

The captain is desperately trying to regain control of the plane.

Butt-Head slams into the cockpit, landing on the control panel facing the captain.

                    CAPTAIN
          Get the hell out of the cockpit!

                    BUTT-HEAD
          Huh huh, you said...

                    CAPTAIN
          NOW!!!

The captain throws Butt-Head back behind him and pulls the plane out of the dive.

EXT. LAS VEGAS AIRPORT - EARLY EVENING

The plane lands.

INT. COCKPIT DOOR - DAY

The flight attendants, shaken, smile at a line of people deplaning. The people are white with fear, some covered with flecks of spilled food and other matter.

19

                    ATTENDANTS
          Bye-bye. Bye-bye. Bye-bye.

They grow silent and still as B&B pass by. Beavis takes the tee-shirt
off his head, coming down from Cornholio.

                    BUTT-HEAD
          Huh huh huh. That was cool.

INT.   TERMINAL/ARRIVAL GATE - DAY

Arriving passengers are greeted. A family is reunited. Two businessmen
walk up to limo drivers holding cards with their names. A reunited
couple hugs.

B&B look around in confusion.

                    BUTT-HEAD
          Uh, huh huh, this is Las Vegas?

                    BEAVIS
          Yeah, heh heh. I thought there'd be
          Casinos and lights and stuff.

People greet and walk away. The place starts to clear out.

One limo driver is left standing. He wears sunglasses and holds a sign
that reads: Beavis and Butt-Head.

B&B look around. Except for the driver, they're alone.

                    BEAVIS (CONT.)
          Hey Butt-Head, why's that guy holding a
          sign?

                    BUTT-HEAD
          Uh... Maybe he's blind...Huh huh, check
          this out.

B&B go up to him. Butt-Head turns around, drops his pants and hangs a
"B.A." at the guy.

                    B&B
          Huh huh huh huh huh huh huh.

                    DRIVER
          Ah, excuse me. You wouldn't know where I
          can find these guys, would ya?

He indicates the sign. Butt-Head turns around and pulls up his pants.
They look and try to read:

                          20

> BUTT-HEAD
> (reads)
> Uh, B...A...U... No, uh, V...

> BEAVIS
> (reads)
> Uh... Buuuuut. Boot. Someone named boot.

> BUTT-HEAD
> (realizes)
> Huh huh. This says Beavis.

> BEAVIS
> And Boot-Head.

> BUTT-HEAD
> That's Butt-Head. Don't you get it,
> Beavis. These dudes have the same name as
> us.

> BEAVIS
> Yeah, we should party.

The limo driver rolls his eyes and walks away.

> DRIVER
> This way, *sirs*.

B&B follow the driver away. Beavis looks around.

> BEAVIS
> So where's those guys?

EXT. MUDDY'S MOTEL ROOM. DAY

HARLAN and ROSS, the two dumb-looking rough-necks that stole B&B's TV are standing outside Muddy's motel room. Harlan knocks on the door.

> ROSS
> Where the hell is he?

> HARLAN
> You sure this is the right place?

Harlan looks through the window and sees the shattered TV. No one's there.

Muddy's four-by-four SQUEALS into the lot and skids to a stop next to Harlan and Ross' van. Muddy gets out, looking really drunk now.

> HARLAN (CONT.)
> You Muddy?

                    MUDDY
                  (slurring)
          You the cops?

                    ROSS
          Uh, no. Earl sent us. You know, to take
          care of your wife...

Muddy grabs Ross by the collar.

                    MUDDY
          What the hell?!...What about those
          other...

                    ROSS
          Huh?

Muddy tosses Ross to the sidewalk and starts back to the four-by-four.

                    MUDDY
          Dammit!!! She did it to me again!!!

                    HARLAN
          Hey, I noticed your TV was broken. You
          wanna by a new one?

Muddy gets in the four-by-four and starts it.

                    MUDDY
          I'm gonna go to Vegas and kill all three
          a' them!

Harlan and Ross seem momentarily confused.

Muddy revs the engine, peels out backwards HITTING THE FRONT OF THE VAN.
This causes B&B's TV and some other loot to spill out the back onto the
sidewalk.

Ross starts to pick it up.

                    HARLAN
          Just leave it. Worthless piece o' crap.

                    ROSS
          Yeah, really. We gotta start stealin' from
          rich people.

EXT.   LAS VEGAS - DAY

MONTAGE SONG BEGINS.

> Note: I would like this to be a well-known band (Red Hot
> Chili Peppers) doing their best imitation of a modern Las
> Vegas Lounge act. I think a song like "What am I gonna do
> with you" by Barry White or something obnoxious like,
> "Bicostal" by Peter Allan would be cool. Or maybe Sinatra's
> "You Make Me Feel So Young" would be best.

The car passes by major hotels and tourist sights, finally pulling up to
a big luxurious hotel and casino.

INT.   HOTEL/CASINO - DAY

Establishing shots. Excitement. Gambling tables going on forever.

ON THE LOUNGE BAND playing the song we've been hearing. They should
vaguely resemble the actual band doing the song.

PAN DOWN Rows of slot machines.

PAN ACROSS DEALERS handling cards and chips.

DOLLY RIGHT UP TO B&B, staring in utter awe.

REVERSE ANGLE REVEALS: They're staring at a huge Roman statue of a bare-
chested woman.

Their faces are blank. They're seeing God. Finally:

                    BUTT-HEAD
          Beavis. This is what it's all about.

                    BEAVIS
                    (speechless)
          Heh heh. Yeah.

EXT.   VEGAS - DUSK

Lights are popping on.

Billboards and signs are lighting up.

The whole strip is coming alive. Pure excitement.

INT.   HOTEL/CASINO - DUSK

ON B&B, still staring at statue.

                         B&B
                       (in awe)
                 Huh huh huh huh huh.

A security guard comes and drags B&B away.

ON THE LOUNGE BAND, continuing the song we've been hearing.

INT.   B&B'S HOTEL ROOM - NIGHT

The door is opened by a bellboy.

                       BELLBOY
                 I'm so sorry about that little
                 misunderstanding. We didn't know you were
                 registered guests. Here's some playing
                 chips compliments of...

Beavis rushes in and grabs the remote which is attached to the night
table. He tries to pull it up and can't.

                       BEAVIS
                 This remote's too heavy!

                       BELLBOY
                 Sir, it's attached to the...

                       BUTT-HEAD
                 Here, dumbass! Let me try.

They both struggle to pull it up. Finally, they fall over backwards.

Annoyed, the bellboy leaves.

INT.   ELEVATOR BANK/9TH FLOOR - NIGHT

The elevator arrives. B&B get on. There's several sophisticated people.
From inside, a computerized FEMALE ELEVATOR VOICE:

                    ELEVATOR VOICE
                 Ninth floor, going down.

                         B&B
                 Huh huh huh huh huh huh.

                       BUTT-HEAD
                 Going down. Huh huh huh.

The sophisticated people look repulsed. The doors close.

INT.   HOTEL/CASINO - NIGHT

MUSIC DIPS DOWN FOR DIALOGUE. B&B step off the elevator and walk among the gambling tables.

Beavis pulls one of the playing chips out of his pocket and bites into it.

> **BEAVIS**
> Ow! These chips suck.

> **BUTT-HEAD**
> What a rip-off. Come on. We gotta find that chick.

Beavis tosses the chip on a roulette table.

ANGLE ON THE WHEEL. The ball lands on 13.

At the table, the DEALER...

> **DEALER**
> 13. We have a winner. (to Beavis) Sir, your chips?

> **BEAVIS**
> I don't want 'em! Keep 'em.

> **DEALER**
> Let it ride!

> **BUTT-HEAD**
> (to dealer)
> Uh... could you help us find a chick?

> **DEALER**
> (uneasy)
> Sir, the casino does not partake in that kind of activity.

The wheel stops.

> **DEALER** (CONT.)
> (amazed)
> 13! Winner!

People oooh and aaah. More gather to watch.

Through the gathering throng comes CHERYL, a hooker.

> **CHERYL**
> Excuse me, boys. Did I hear you say you're looking for a date?

B&B freeze, shocked.

> **CHERYL** (CONT.)
> I'm Cheryl, and I can show you a real fine
> time.

B&B don't move. The dealer rolls again.

> **CHERYL** (CONT.)
> A time you'll remember for the rest of
> your lives, if you know what I mean.

> **DEALER**
> (to Beavis)
> Sir, do you want your chips?

> **BEAVIS**
> No, Dammit! I don't want any chips!

> **DEALER**
> Let it ride.

Cheryl puts her hands on their thighs.

> **CHERYL**
> What say we three go up to your room, take
> off our clothes and just see what comes
> up.

B&B's eyes open wide.

> **BUTT-HEAD**
> Huh huh huh huh huh huh.

> **BEAVIS**
> Uh... Uh...

The wheel stops.

> **DEALER**
> 14. No winners.

> **CHERYL**
> Hmmmm. Oh well.

She leaves. People scatter. B&B are left alone. Staring.

> **BUTT-HEAD**
> Huh huh huh. That chick was talking about
> doing it.

                              BEAVIS
                Heh heh. This is the best night of our
                lives.

WIDE SHOT. B&B just stand, laughing.

MUSIC FADES BACK UP...

INT.   HOTEL LOUNGE - NIGHT

ANGLE ON THE BAND, continuing the song.

Tourists watch from tables - decidedly not rocking out.

B&B dance alone near the stage, doing the "butt-knocker."

INT.   HOTEL OFFICE - NIGHT

A WOMAN ATTENDANT answers the phone.

                      WOMAN ATTENDANT
                Good evening. Room service. How may I help
                you?

From the phone...

                          B&B
                       (on phone)
                Huh huh huh huh huh.

The woman's disturbed.

                      WOMAN ATTENDANT
                Hello... Hello...

INT. HOTEL/CASINO - NIGHT

B&B try to climb up and grab the gigantic boobs of the statue. Butt-Head
falls, knocks Beavis off and they both hit the floor hard.

INT.   B&B'S HOTEL ROOM - NIGHT

Beavis is on the phone in the main room. Butt-Head sits on the toilet
and speaks from the phone in the bathroom.

                       BUTT-HEAD
                Uh, huh huh, I'd like to be serviced... in
                my room.

                          B&B
                Huh huh huh huh huh huh.

INT.   HOTEL LOUNGE - NIGHT

B&B keep dancing as the famous BAND plays the MONTAGE SONG which ENDS.

EXT.   VEGAS - DAWN

Sun rise.

The song rings out.

INT. B&B'S ROOM - MORNING

Beavis is picking up the night table by the remote attached to it and moving the whole thing.

Butt-Head approaches a door next to the bed.

> **BUTT-HEAD**
> Uh, I wonder where this door goes to.

Beavis comes over to check it out. Butt-Head opens the door. It's one of those double doors to the next room.

Butt-Head tries to open the second door, jiggling it.

> Suddenly, the door opens. Someone reaches out and pulls B&B inside. It's DALLAS, the girl Muddy sent them after.

> INT.   DALLAS' SUITE/MAIN ROOM - CONTINUOUS

She has them pinned against the wall. DALLAS is hot, clad in tight leather, tattooed, pierced, sexy.

> **BEAVIS**
> (excited)
> Hey Butt-Head, it's her! Heh heh.

> **DALLAS**
> All right, who are ya? C.I.A.? F.B.I.?
> A.T.F.?

> **BUTT-HEAD**
> Uh... Hey baby. Are we like, doing it?

> **BEAVIS**
> Me first!

> **DALLAS**
> You got two seconds!

> **BUTT-HEAD**
> Uh, huh huh. Is that gonna be enough time?

Dallas grabs Butt-Head by the shirt.

>   **DALLAS**
> Who sent ya?

>   **BUTT-HEAD**
> Uh, huh huh, this fat dude. He said we
> could do you. And he was gonna pay us.

>   **DALLAS**
> Muddy! Sonofabitch! Hold it. What's he
> payin' ya?

>   **BUTT-HEAD**
> Uh, ten uh...

>   **DALLAS**
> Ten grand? That cheap-ass.... I got a
> better deal for ya. I'll double it. I'll
> pay ya twenty if you go back there and do
> mah husband.

>   **BUTT-HEAD**
> Uh, you want us to do a guy? Huh huh. No
> way.

>   **BEAVIS**
>   (considering it)
> Umm,... I don't know Butt-Head. That is a
> lot of money... Maybe if we close our eyes
> and pretend he's a chick...

Butt-Head SMACKS Beavis, bringing him to his senses.

From outside, SOUND of a police siren. Dallas goes to the window. The
place is being surrounded by police and plain black cars.

>   **DALLAS**
>   (panics)
> Damn! You boys, you wait right there.

Dallas goes into the next room and closes the door.

B&B look at each other. They start to take their pants off.

>   **BUTT-HEAD**
> Huh huh huh. I'm ready for love.

>   **BEAVIS**
> Me first! Me first!

INT.   DALLAS' SUITE/OTHER ROOM - DAY

Dallas gets binoculars from her bag and scouts outside.

Her P.O.V. REVEALS dozens of police and A.T.F. cars. The hotel's surrounded.

As Dallas looks around, she spots a tour bus across the street. On the side: "Dream America Tours." Dallas quickly dials the phone.

> **DALLAS**
> (to phone)
> Gimme the number for Dream America Tours.
> (pause) Right.

Dallas dials again, crossing to the door to peek out at B&B - both standing in their underwear, waiting. Beavis picks his nose. Dallas closes the door again.

> **DALLAS** (CONT.)
> (to phone)
> Yeah, you got a bus leaving today? (pause)
> Five minutes? Where's it goin'? (listens)
> Washington, D.C.? (mulls it over) Perfect.
> (a look back to the other room) Gimme two
> tickets.

INT.   DALLAS' SUITE/MAIN ROOM - DAY

B&B are in their underwear. Butt-Head sits at the edge of the bed. Beavis tries to pull the remote off the table.

Dallas enters, sees this sight, and shuts off the TV. She looms over Butt-Head.

> **BUTT-HEAD**
> So, uh, huh huh. Are we gonna score now?

> **BEAVIS**
> Me first!

> **BUTT-HEAD**
> Forget it, bunghole!

B&B start to wrestle. Dallas sees Beavis' pants.

> **DALLAS**
> (realizing)
> Score? You boys wanna....?

Butt-Head grabs Beavis' neck.

30

BEAVIS
Ow, let go, Butt-Head!

BUTT-HEAD
Huh huh huh.

She picks up the pants, getting an idea.

DALLAS
You wait here.

She takes the pants into the next room. B&B keep wrestling.

BEAVIS
Me first.

BUTT-HEAD
Huh huh. No way, dude.

INT.   DALLAS' SUITE/OTHER ROOM - DAY

TIGHT ON her black satchel. From it she lifts a delicate electronic device, the X-5 *unit*, about the size of a credit card. An LED light blinks.

Using her switchblade, she cuts a whole in the back seam of Beavis' pants, creating a natural pocket. She carefully slides the *unit* in.

INT. DALLAS' SUITE/MAIN ROOM - DAY

B&B's fight escalates. Butt-Head picks up a LAMP and throws it at Beavis. It hits the wall and SHATTERS. Beavis charges Butt-Head.

INT. DALLAS' SUITE/OTHER ROOM - DAY

Dallas is licking a piece of thread. She quickly and expertly threads a needle and then starts to sew the electronic device into the inside back of Beavis' pants. She suddenly wrinkles her nose as if she has smelled something.

She holds up the pants to the light. Inside, the shadow of the *unit*.

INT.   DALLAS'S SUITE/MAIN ROOM - DAY

B&B fight wildly. Dallas enters and clears her throat. B&B freeze.

FULL ON DALLAS, posed sexily, seductive.

DALLAS
Don't wear yourselves out, boys. Save some
energy for me.

                    B&B
Huh huh huh huh huh huh.

                 BUTT-HEAD
This is it, Beavis. Huh huh. We're finally
gonna score.

                  BEAVIS
Heh heh. Thank God.

                   DALLAS
I'm gonna do it with both of ya.

                    B&B
              (uncontrollable)
Huh huh huh huh huh huh huh huh huh huh
huh huh huh huh huh.

Dallas clears her throat to get their attention. And again.

                   DALLAS
(sexy) Boys... (shouts) Boys!!!

Silence.

              DALLAS (CONT.)
But first, you hafta do a little job for
me. (touches seductively) Would you like
to do a job for me?

Silence. They're in shock.

              DALLAS (CONT.)
Here's what it is. I want ya ta take a bus
ta Washington, D.C. That's all. And when
ya get there, I'll be waitin'. You're
gonna make a whole lotta money. (In their
faces) And I'm gonna give you everything!

                    B&B
              (near comatose)
Huh huh huh huh huh huh huh.

                   DALLAS
Until then... (tosses Beavis' pants in his
face) Keep your pants on.

She looks back to the window, now all business.

              DALLAS (CONT.)
OK guys, time to move out.

INT.   HOTEL LOBBY/FRONT DOOR - DAY

A.T.F. agents enter and spread out. We see several agents go up the stairs.

INT. DALLAS' ROOM/DOORWAY - DAY

> **DALLAS**
> Remember, Washington, D.C. You'll get more
> money than you ever dreamed of. And you'll
> get me.

She kisses them both seductively.

> **DALLAS** (CONT.)
> (urgent)
> Your bus is downstairs. Get going.

She shuts the door, leaving B&B outside. Nearby, a maid with her cart passes by.

B&B stare, frozen for a beat, then go running for the elevator.

ANGLE AROUND THE CORNER, out of B&B's view. Just as the elevator doors shut, dozens of federal agents with guns rush in and kick open Dallas' door.

EXT.   HOTEL/CASINO - DAY

More Feds and police enter.

ANGLE ON B&B, walking past, oblivious to all else. As he walks away, Beavis rubs his butt.

> **B&B**
> Huh huh huh huh huh.

> **BUTT-HEAD**
> This is gonna be cool. Huh huh.

They walk to the tour bus across the street.

INT.   TOUR BUS - DAY

B&B walk down the aisle, Beavis rubbing his butt. Most seats are taken by senior citizens.

Up ahead, two vacant seats. B&B fight to get in first.

> **BUTT-HEAD**
> No way butt-hole! I want the window.

BEAVIS
Cut it out butt-hole!

A VOICE
Why don't you take turns?

They turn. It's Martha, the woman from the plane, sitting across the aisle.

BEAVIS
Hey, Butt-Head, it's that slut from the plane!

MARTHA
Why it's you two. How'd ya do in Vegas?

BEAVIS
Uh, we didn't score yet.

MARTHA
Sorry to hear that. Me, I took a beating.

BUTT-HEAD
Cool, huh huh huh.

MARTHA
That's why I'm bussing it across America. I'm so glad you're here. (to man in next seat) Jim, I want you to meet two nice boys.

JIM, an old guy, wakes up and looks over.

MARTHA (CONT.)
This is Travis and Bob... What's your last name, dear?

BUTT-HEAD
Uh... Head? Huh huh. My first name's Butt. Huh huh huh.

JIM
Pleased ta meet ya, Mr. Head.

All the seniors around turn to meet them.

MARTHA
Meet Sylvia. And Elloise and Sam. And Ed. And Doreen.

BUTT-HEAD
Are you guys sluts too? Huh huh huh.

EXT.   TOUR BUS - DAY

It takes off.

We PAN back to the hotel as Muddy arrives in a cab.

INT.   HALLWAY OUTSIDE DALLAS' ROOM - DAY

DRAMATIC REVEAL of AGENT RYAN FLEMMING entering the hallway. He's an A.T.F. honcho, powerful, hard-ass. Looks like an Oliver North-type. Sounds something like Fred Thompson. He walks with his assistant, AGENT BORK and another agent.

They find Dallas' room and enter.

INT.   DALLAS' HOTEL ROOM - DAY

Dallas sits calmly, confident, as agents tear apart the room.

                    FLEMMING
          So, are you going to tell us where it is
          or am I going to have to have Agent Hurley
          over there give you another cavity search?

ANGLE ON AGENT HURLEY a tough, stocky woman.

                    DALLAS
          Ooh is that a promise?

                    FLEMMING
          Look Mrs. Scum, we know who you are. Tell
          her Bork.

                    BORK
          Dallas Grimes. Married to Muddy Grimes.
          You run a mom and pop arms smuggling ring.

He tosses some photos of her and Muddy.

                    DALLAS
          Oh, you got my bad side.

Bork hands Flemming another file. Flemming checks it.

                    FLEMMING
          Three days ago you pulled a job at the
          Army Research Facility in Hadley, Nevada -
          where you stole... (reads) The X-5 unit.
          Now we happen to know you had the unit
          with you when you checked in here, so why
          don't you be a good girl and tell us where
          it is.

                    DALLAS
          You gonna charge me with anything? (pause)
          I didn't think so. You wanna let me go now
          or wait 'till my lawyer files a wrongful
          arrest.

                     BORK
                  (aside to Flemming)
          We got nothing, Chief. We tore the place
          apart. We can only legally hold her for
          another couple of hours.

                   FLEMMING
                  (aside to Bork)
          Dammit! (slams fist down) Where's that
          damn *unit*??!!

EXT.   HOOVER DAM - DAY

The bus parks.

INT.   TOUR BUS - DAY

B&B are excited.

                    BEAVIS
          Heh heh. We're in Washington!

                   BUTT-HEAD
          Huh huh. We're gonna score now.

                    MARTHA
          Actually, we're at the Hoover Dam.

Martha walks on down the aisle.

                   BUTT-HEAD
          Damn, huh huh.

                    BEAVIS
          Yeah, heh heh. Damn right!

They follow the seniors out of the bus. Beavis rubs his butt.

EXT.   THE ROAD - DAY

     Dallas drives by in a slick car.

     INT.   DALLAS' CAR - DAY

     She adjusts her rearview mirror to observe a Fed car
     following her. She smiles.

INT.   HOOVER DAM - DAY

B&B and the seniors are on a tour through the giant
basement. B&B talk and approach the HOOVER GUIDE, speaking
nearby.

                         BEAVIS
          So, like, where is she?

                         BUTT-HEAD
                    (looks around)
          Yeah, really.

                         HOOVER GUIDE
          Over 40 thousand cubic tons of concrete
          were used in the construction of the
          Hoover Dam.

                         B&B
          Huh huh huh huh huh huh.

                         HOOVER GUIDE
          From top to bottom, the this dam is 51
          stories.

                         BEAVIS
          Uh, huh huh, excuse me. Is this a God
          Damn?

                         B&B
          Huh huh huh huh huh.

They follow the tour into the next room.

INT.   HOOVER DAM/OBSERVATION ROOM - DUSK

A glass wall separates this from the master control room. There, two
technicians are on watch. Banks of monitors show the water and pipes
from various angles.

B&B are the last in. Beavis rubs his aching butt. The guide is already
speaking.

                         HOOVER GUIDE
          ... Generates over 6000 gigawatts of
          electricity, all passing through this
          control room. This way.

The tour moves on.

                         BUTT-HEAD
          This is dumb, let's find that chick.

                    BEAVIS
        Yeah, heh heh, enough'a this crap.

They walk back from where they came.

Through the glass wall, we see the two control room technicians heading
out.

                  BEAVIS (CONT.)
        Check it out Butt-Head, TV!

                   BUTT-HEAD
        Cool! Huh huh huh.

INT.   HOOVER DAM/HALL OUTSIDE CONTROL ROOM DOOR - DAY

SOUND of air compression as this secure door opens. The two technicians
walk out.

They walk away, not seeing that behind them, B&B approach the control
room door. They enter just before the door closes. SOUND of air
compression locks.

INT.   A.T.F. HEADQUARTERS/FLEMMING'S OFFICE - DUSK

Agent Bork knocks and enters.

                    FLEMMING
        Talk ta me, Bork.

                      BORK
        Chief, we found a witness that says he saw
        two teenagers leaving Dallas' room shortly
        before we arrived.

                    FLEMMING
        Did you give him a full cavity search?

                      BORK
                  (confused)
        Ah, the witness?

                    FLEMMING
        Yes. You can never be too careful Bork.

                      BORK
        Well sir, I didn't really think it was
        necessary. You see we have a picture of
        them from the elevator security cam. Here,
        have a look.

TIGHT ON PICTURE. A still of B&B laughing on the elevator.

BORK (CONT.)
They look like a couple of kids chief.

FLEMMING
Bork, don't you realize what kids today
are capable of? Don't you read the papers?

Suddenly the lights blink on and off. All three men look up.

INT.   HOOVER DAM/CONTROL ROOM - DUSK

We see a bank of TV monitors, video of water, turbines etc. Beavis is
rubbing his butt against a switch on the console, causing the lights to
blink on and off.

BUTT-HEAD
Beavis, huh huh, what'er you doing?

BEAVIS
My butt's bothering me!

BUTT-HEAD
You should kick your butt's ass. Huh huh
huh.

Butt-Head looks at the bank of monitors - all showing water.

BUTT-HEAD (CONT.)
Dammit, all they have is shows about
water.

BEAVIS
That sucks. Heh heh. They need some shows
about fire! Change the channel.

BUTT-HEAD
Uh...

Butt-Head starts randomly hitting controls everywhere while Beavis rubs
his butt against a computer keypad.

TIGHT ON CONTROL: "Main Water Release Valve". Butt-Head turns it. An
alarm sounds.

BEAVIS
Yeah, turn it up! Louder! Heh heh.

INT.   DAM DOORS - DUSK

An alarm sounds. Giant doors open, causing water to start to flood
through the gates.

INT.   HOOVER DAM/CONTROL ROOM - DUSK

Butt-Head presses more buttons. His hand is near the biggest switch for: "Master Station Control".

> **BUTT-HEAD**
> (reads sign)
> Uh... Mas... Ter... Huh huh. Mastur<u>ba</u>tion, huh huh.

Butt-Head throws the switch. Lights go out. SOUND of generators grinding to a halt.

INT.   HOOVER DAM/MACHINE ROOM - DUSK

Machinery stops suddenly and large support beams break. A disaster.

INT.   HOOVER DAM/CONTROL ROOM - DUSK

SOUND of twisted, grinding metal, loud alarms.

> **BUTT-HEAD**
> Uh...

ON ONE OF THE MONITORS, we see a small electrical fire.

> **BEAVIS**
> Yeah, fire! Fire! FIRE!!!

EXT.   HOOVER DAM - DUSK

The lights go out.

EXT.   VEGAS STRIP - DUSK

In succession, one set of lights after another goes out. The famous strip goes dark.

INT.   A.T.F. HEADQUARTERS/FLEMMING'S OFFICE - DUSK

The lights go dead.

> **FLEMMING**
> The hell's going on?

INT.   HOSPITAL OPERATING ROOM/VEGAS - DUSK

A surgeon just makes an incision as the lights go out.

> **SURGEON**
> Whoooooops.

40

EXT.   CAMPGROUND - DUSK

Marcy Anderson hammers the last peg in for their tent. Tom checks the
stew on the fire and looks around.

                         TOM
               I'll tell ya, it doesn't get any better
               than this. This here is God's country.
               Unspoiled and...

A rumbling interrupts him. He and Marcy turn to see:

A wall of water, heading for them.

                         TOM (CONT.)
               Aaaaghhh!!!...

They're smashed by the flood.

EXT.   HOOVER DAM - DUSK

Mass chaos. Traffic jams. Honking horns. People shouting.

ANGLE ON B&B AND THE SENIORS, about to get on the bus.

                         BUTT-HEAD
               That was boring. Huh huh.

                         BEAVIS
               Yeah, it's just the same thing over and
               over again.

                         BUTT-HEAD
               Uh... We can't leave Washington 'till we
               find that chick.

                         MARTHA
               Oh, we're a long ways from Washington Bob.
               This is the Hoover Dam.

Martha gets on the bus. HOLD ON B&B.

                         BEAVIS
               Damn! Heh heh hmm heh.

They get on the bus.

INT.   VEGAS HOTEL/CASINO - DUSK

Mayhem. People scream in the dark. Some steal chips and run.

41

ANGLE TO SIDE, where Muddy has the Concierge by the neck.

                    CONCIERGE
          I swear, that's all I know! They got on
          that tour bus. It was probably heading
          west. Please...

Muddy slams him against the wall and walks away.

                    MUDDY
          I'm gonna kill 'em!

EXT.   HOOVER DAM - DUSK

The doors close on the tour bus. It pulls out and drives away.

EXT.   SIDE OF ROAD - DUSK

At her car, Dallas watches the bus from a distance, then lays down her
binoculars, satisfied.

                    DALLAS
          You boys better show up.

With a look at the Fed car behind her, She gets in her car and drives
down a different road.

EXT.   ROAD - DUSK

The bus heads off into the desert.

DISSOLVE TO:

EXT.   HOOVER DAM - MORNING

Police cars everywhere. Fire engines. Reporters. News helicopters.
Disaster.

Several A.T.F. cars pull up. Flemming and several of his agents get out
and head immediately for the dam.

INT.   HOOVER DAM/CONFERENCE ROOM - MORNING

TIGHT ON A TV MONITOR. It shows B&B at the Hoover Dam controls the eve
before, shot on surveillance camera. Frame freezes. B&B looking
particularly stupid.

REVEAL Flemming's there with his agents. Flemming leans forward.

                    FLEMMING
          You see what I see, Bork?

                    BORK
          I see it. I don't get it.

                    FLEMMING
          You got half the state looking for ya -
          how do you get away?

                    BORK
                    (realizes)
          Cut the power!

                    FLEMMING
          Damn right. Bork, we're dealing with real
          pros here. My opinion, terrorists...
          What's the scoop on that stolen *unit?*

                    BORK
          Well, sir it's not good. (to an assistant)
          Roll the tape... The X-5 unit is a new
          top-secret biological weapon, a manmade
          virus...

ON MONITOR. The device that was put in back of Beavis' pants.

                    BORK (CONT.)
          The deadliest known to man. It could wipe
          out five states in five days. It can be
          activated by simply entering the right
          code. Here's what happened when it was
          tested on a group of Army recruits..

ON THE MONITOR. Army recruits coughing up black gunk, Rolling around in
pain on stretchers, dying. Grotesque (but funny).

                    FLEMMING
          Jesus Jumped-Up Christ! If this were to
          fall into the wrong hands...

                    BORK
          It gets worse. The *unit* wasn't finished.
          It has a flaw - the casing. If hit hard
          enough, it could break open, releasing the
          virus.

A murmuring through the room. Flemming rises and holds up a picture of
B&B.

                    FLEMMING
          Okay People, as of right now these are the
          most dangerous men in America. I want
          these faces in front of every fed and two-
          bit sheriff within a thousand miles. The
          orders are dead or alive. Let's just pray
          that nothing hits that *unit*.

INT.   TOUR BUS - DAY

TIGHT ON Beavis' butt, as Butt-Head KICKS IT REPEATEDLY.

                    BEAVIS
          Ow! Cut it out Butt-Head.

                    BUTT-HEAD
          Huh huh. Get out of the way, Beavis, I
          wanna sit by the window. Huh huh.

                    BEAVIS
          Ow! I'll kick your butt!

                    BUTT-HEAD
          Huh huh. You mean like this?

Butt-Head keeps kicking.

ANGLE ON THE DRIVER UP FRONT.

                    DRIVER
          Okay, people, next stop, Grand Canyon.

He guns it.

EXT.   TOUR BUS - DAY

It takes off down the road.

MONTAGE SONG BEGINS. (Maybe White Zombie doing something like, "Born to
be Wild")

INSERT: A RED LINE snakes across a map to Grand Canyon.

EXT.   GRAND CANYON - DAY

Gorgeous. Our seniors and others take pictures and stare in awe. Some
hold hands. One crosses herself.

ANGLE ON B&B, nearby, also staring in awe. REVEAL they're watching a
jackass take a dump.

                    B&B
          Huh huh huh huh huh.

44

                    BEAVIS
          The poop's coming out of the ass of the
          ass. Heh heh heh.

                    BUTT-HEAD
          Huh huh. It's coming out of the ass, but
          it's also coming out of the ass <u>of</u> the
          ass.

INT.   A.T.F. HEADQUARTERS - DAY

TIGHT ON PHOTO OF B&B, going out on the wire.

INT.   A POLICE STATION - DAY

TIGHT ON COP getting the photo off a machine.

INT.   A POST OFFICE - DAY

TIGHT ON B&B's PHOTO as it's pinned to the wall.

INT.   DRIVING TOUR BUS - DAY

PAN across seniors showing off pictures of their grandchildren.

Pan stops on B&B showing off a picture of Dallas to a senior. Butt-Head
does the "finger-in-hole" fornication gesture as they LAUGH
suggestively.

EXT.   SIDE OF ROAD - DAY

Flemming reads a map strewn on his hood. He turns to Bork to give
orders. Bork repeats them into his radio. Several cars pull out.

INSERT: A RED LINE snakes across a map to Utah.

EXT.   SALT LAKE CITY - DAY

Martha and the seniors pose in front of a classic Salt Lake City view. A
sign nearby reads "Welcome to Salt Lake City."

REVERSE ANGLE shows B&B, taking their picture.

P.O.V. OF CAMERA shows Butt-Head's hand covering half the lens. Framing
is crooked and way off. Click and FREEZE.

EXT.   SIDE OF HIGHWAY - DAY

Middle of nowhere. Confused, Martha is taking a picture.

REVERSE ANGLE shows B&B, posing by the road sign: Baggs, Wyoming.

                              B&B
               Huh huh huh huh huh huh.

P.O.V. OF CAMERA, showing B&B laughing.

INSERT: A RED LINE snakes across the map to Wyoming.

CROSS-DISSOLVE BETWEEN THE BUS AND THE SIGHTS IT PASSES:

EXT.   FLAMING GORGE, WYOMING - DAY

A classic view of a powerful gorge.

REVERSE SHOWS THE TOUR BUS driving by. Martha and the seniors rush to
the windows to stare in awe.

EXT.   GRAND TETON, WYOMING - DAY

A classic view of the huge peaks.

REVERSE SHOWS THE TOUR BUS driving by. More seniors rush to the windows
to see.

EXT.   YELLOWSTONE PARK, WYOMING - DAY

A spectacular view of Yellowstone Lake and the Rockies.

REVERSE SHOWS THE TOUR BUS. Seniors staring in awe.

PAN over to another window. B&B press their BARE ASSES against the
window.

EXT.   YELLOWSTONE/OLD FAITHFUL - DAY

MONTAGE SONG ENDS.

A RANGER/GUIDE stands in front of the seniors talking about the geyser.
B&B are towards the front, off to one side.

                         RANGER
                       (a la Carl Sagan)
               There are over *two hundred* active geysers
               in Yellowstone park alone. Old Faithful
               here is one of the largest. During an
               eruption the water can reach as high as
               two hundred feet!...

                       BUTT-HEAD
               So?

                                RANGER
                          (ignoring Butt-Head)
                  It shoots out over *twelve thousand* gallons
                  of water in a single eruption...

                                BEAVIS
                  That's not that much.

                                BUTT-HEAD
                  Yeah really. Let's get outta here Beavis.
                  Huh huh huh. This sucks.

B&B walk off as the flustered ranger leads the seniors to some benches
where they wait for the geyser to erupt.

EXT.   YELLOWSTONE/OLD FAITHFUL - LATER

The geyser erupts. The seniors watch in sheer awe.

                                MARTHA
                    It's...incredible...!

INT. OLD FAITHFUL/MEN'S BATHROOM - DAY

B&B stare ahead in similar awe.

                                BUTT-HEAD
                    It's incredible!... Huh huh huh.

REVEAL they're standing before the urinals. Butt-Head moves to the side,
tripping a motion detector which makes the urinal AUTOMATICALLY FLUSH.

                                BEAVIS
                    Whoa! That's amazing! Heh heh heh.

They start moving from urinal to urinal, causing all to flush.

EXT.   OLD FAITHFUL/PARKING AREA - DAY

A BIT LATER.

The bus idles. The last senior climbs onboard.

The driver looks around impatiently. He checks his watch.

                                DRIVER
                    I can't wait forever.

INT.   OLD FAITHFUL/RANGER'S OFFICE - DAY

The ranger/guide enters and checks off a chart on a bulletin board near
B&B's "wanted" photo.

Suddenly the guide sees B&B's photo, then, out the window, the bus closing its door and pulling away.

                    RANGER
          Oh my God!

The guide picks up the phone.

INT. VISITOR CENTER/MEN'S ROOM - DAY

B&B go back and forth, "playing" the urinals, passing hands, heads, whole bodies in front of the motion detectors.

                     B&B
          Huh huh huh huh.

Finally, Butt-Head pauses.

                  BUTT-HEAD
          This is the coolest thing I have ever
          seen.

EXT. SIDE OF A ROAD - DAY

Flemming is on the radio. Bork runs up.

                    BORK
          Chief, we got 'em! They're on a senior
          citizens tour bus going east on I-40.

EXT. OLD FAITHFUL/PARKING LOT - DAY

B&B get on a bus that looks completely different than the tour bus.

INT. DIFFERENT BUS - DAY

TIGHT ON B&B. Butt-Head looks around.

                  BUTT-HEAD
          Uh... Is this the right bus?

                   BEAVIS
          You mean there's more than one?

A WIDER SHOT REVEALS it's a bus full of nuns. B&B look around and see this.

                  BUTT-HEAD
          Huh huh huh. Hey Beavis. We're on a bus
          with chicks.

                   BEAVIS
          Heh hmm heh heh.

Butt-Head turns to the nun next to him.

                    BUTT-HEAD
            Hey, baby.

The nun looks disturbed as the bus takes off.

EXT. I-40/SIDE OF THE ROAD - DAY

The tour bus is stopped. Like P.O.W.'s, the seniors stand with hands on heads. Agents search the bus.

ANGLE ON LINE OF SENIORS. Flemming walks nearby and is told:

                    BORK
            They're not on the bus.

Flemming looks the seniors over.

                    FLEMMING
                (re: seniors)
            These people know something. I want full
            cavity searches. Everyone. Go deep on 'em.

Hurley and two agents grab the nearest senior and drag him away.

                    FLEMMING (CONT.)
            I tell you Bork, these guys are smart.
            Damn smart. They're probably a hundred
            miles away by now.

Behind Flemming, an agent waves on traffic including B&B's new bus. As it pulls past, B&B hang B.A.'s. Flemming doesn't see.

MONTAGE SONG BEGINS:

INSERT: A RED LINE snakes through a map, pretty much retracing the route B&B took north. Down into Utah.

INT.   BUS - DAY

A nun strums a guitar and sings. Butt-Head head-bangs. The nuns around look uneasy.

Nearby another nun reads the bible to Beavis.

                    BEAVIS
            Hey, Butt-Head, this book kicks ass!
            There's this talking snake and a naked
            chick and then this dude puts a leaf on
            his schlong! Heh heh heh.

The nun next to Beavis is disgusted.

INSERT: A RED LINE snakes down through Colorado.

One of the nuns is trying to teach B&B the sign of the cross.

Butt-Head moves his hand up, down, left and then swings his hand to the far right SMACKING Beavis.

INT.   ROADSIDE RESTAURANT - DAY

Sitting before a long table, the nuns close their eyes and pray, hands clasped together.

PAN THE ROW to B&B who's hands are clasped together and interlocked as they do the incredibly juvenile 'peek at the vagina' trick.

                         B&B
               Huh huh huh huh huh huh.

INSERT: A RED LINE snakes through a map to Rancho Taos, New Mexico.

EXT. MISSION OF ST. FRANCIS OF ASSISI CHURCH - DAY

A beautiful old adobe-style church. Nuns exit the bus, excited, followed by B&B who look around.

The nuns walk into a visitor center. B&B walk right into the church.

INT. CHURCH - DAY

In a WIDE SHOT we see B&B walk in, look around and head for the CONFESSION BOOTHS.

                       BEAVIS
            Check it out Butt-Head, porta-potties.

                     BUTT-HEAD
               Cool, huh huh.

B&B each enter a confession both on the priest's side.

INT. ST. FRANCIS CHURCH - LATER

WIDE EST. SHOT shows that a confessional service has begun.

INT. ST. FRANCIS CHURCH/CONFESSION BOOTH - DAY

We see a man nervously confessing. This seems difficult for him.

                         MAN
                    (about to cry)
            Forgive me Father for I have sinned.
            I,...I...I slept with a woman, and...

From the priest's side of the confessional we hear Butt-Head.
The man can't see him.

> **BUTT-HEAD** (O.S.)
> Huh huh huh, really? Was she naked?

> **MAN**
> Well, yes Father. Please forgive me. I...

> **BUTT-HEAD** (O.S.)
> Cool, huh huh huh. Could you like, see her
> boobs?

ANGLE INSIDE ANOTHER CONFESSIONAL

> **MAN #2**
> (confused)
> How many Hail Marys?

> **BEAVIS** (O.S.)
> A thousand! Yeah, heh heh hmm. And I want
> you to hit yourself. Right now!

> **MAN #2**
> Now?!

> **BEAVIS** (O.S.)
> Yeah! Heh heh hmm heh. DO IT!

From outside the confession booth, we hear the sound of a SMACK.

> **BEAVIS** (O.S./CONT.)
> Harder! Heh heh. Again! Heh heh. You need
> to straighten up!

EXT. ST. FRANCIS CHURCH - DAY

As B&B board the bus they are STRUCK BY LIGHTNING.

INSERT: A RED LINE snakes further down into Arizona.

EXT.   PETRIFIED FOREST VISITOR'S CENTER - DAY

This establishes.

INT.   PETRIFIED FOREST VISITOR'S CENTER - DAY

B&B stare at an exhibit, riveted. The nuns watch them. A recording
plays.

> **RECORDING** (V.O.)
> Welcome to the Petrified Forest. The
> world's largest sight of petrified wood.

B&B
Huh huh huh huh wood.

The Mother Superior makes a signal the other nuns were waiting for. They all rush back to the bus, leaving B&B behind.

RECORDING (V.O.)
You may wonder, how can wood get so hard?

B&B
Huh huh huh huh huh huh.

Through the window, we see the bus drive away.

ANGLE ON OLD RANGER behind a counter, looking at B&B. He sees their A.T.F. photo nearby and reaches for a phone.

EXT.   PETRIFIED FOREST VISITOR'S CENTER - DAY

MONTAGE SONG ENDS

B&B step outside. Nearby, a tourist car pulls up.

BEAVIS
Hey, where'd those chicks go?

BUTT-HEAD
Uh... I think you scared them off.

BEAVIS
This sucks. What are we doing here?
Weren't we suppost'a go to Washington and
score or something?

From the car, a tourist couple heads into the building.

BUTT-HEAD
(to couple)
Uh, do you know where Washington is?

TOURIST MAN
Yeah, 'bout 2000 miles that way.

He points to the desert, then continues into the building.

BUTT-HEAD
Cool. Huh huh huh.

B&B walk off into the desert.

52

EXT.   PETRIFIED FOREST TOURIST CENTER - LATER

The place is crawling with A.T.F. Flemming walks out with Bork and the
OLD RANGER.

>   **FLEMMING**
>   Didn't see which way they went. Didn't see
>   their vehicle. I don't suppose you tried
>   to stop them?

>   **OLD RANGER**
>   The most dangerous guys in America? Not
>   me, Sonny. I make nine dollars an hour.

>   **FLEMMING**
>   National security is the responsibility of
>   every American. Bork...

>   **BORK**
>   Cavity search...?

>   **FLEMMING**
>   Deep and hard.

Agents lead the old Ranger away.

>   **FLEMMING** (CONT.)
>   (to Bork)
>   They're not gonna get away this time. I
>   want roadblocks. Every road outta here for
>   two hundred miles.

EXT.   ROAD - DAY

IN MONTAGE SHOTS:

A.T.F. agents put up roadblocks.

Agents load guns.

Agents pile up sandbags and prepare for battle.

EXT.   DESERT - DAY

WIDE SHOT. A wasteland. Scorching desert heat. B&B, small in frame, look
lost. They're parched, weak.

>   **BEAVIS**
>   This sucks. It's all hot and stuff.

>   **BUTT-HEAD**
>   This desert is stupid. They need to put a
>   drinking fountain out here.

BEAVIS
Yeah or like a Seven-Eleven or
something... Are we almost there?

BUTT-HEAD
Uh, probably like, another five minutes or
something.

ANGLE FROM OVERHEAD. Lost, alone, B&B wobble like they haven't long to
live. Overhead, vultures circle.

ANGLE ON B&B, exhausted, spent. Staring ahead, Butt-Head suddenly sees
something.

BUTT-HEAD (CONT.)
Whoa! Check it out!

Beavis clears his eyes and sees it too.

B&B
Yes! Yes! Huh huh huh.

Excited, saved, they rush weakly forward.

B&B'S P.O.V. REVEALS they rush to: A GIANT BIG SCREEN TV.

BEAVIS
Turn it on! Turn it on!

As they get closer it disappears — just a mirage.

BUTT-HEAD
Uh....

BEAVIS
Dammit!!!! Dammit!!!!

ANGLE ON SUN, brightening. The FRAME WHITES OUT.

EXT.   ROADBLOCK - DAY

Cars are backed up into the horizon.

The car up front is waved on. Up next: Tom and Marcy. An agent steps
over and shows the picture of B&B.

TOM
Something wrong, Officer?

AGENT
Sir, we're looking for these two
fugitives.

ANDERSON SQUINTS to see.

HIS P.O.V. REVEALS the photo out of focus.

                    ANDERSON
            Why I'll be danged. It's those boys been
            whackin' off in my camper...

                      AGENT
            You saw these two?

                    ANDERSON
            I sure did. They were whackin' off in my
            tool shed. Then whackin' off in my camper.
            I never seen so much whackin' off.

The agent steps back and shouts into his walkie-talkie:

                      AGENT
            Blue Den this is post nine! I have
            positive ID!! (to Tom) Sir, I'm gonna have
            to ask you and your wife to step out of
            the vehicle.

                    ANDERSON
            Well you see, me and the missus are on our
            on our way to Washington. We got this
            schedule...

The agent pulls his gun and orders:

                      AGENT
            Now!!!!

EXT.   SIDE OF HIGHWAY/JUST OFF ROADBLOCK - DAY

A BIT LATER. Agents swarm over Tom's camper, turning everything upside,
pulling out dishes, trashing everything.

                      TOM
                   (furious)
            Now wait right there. You're dealing with
            a veteran of two foreign wars. <u>They're</u> the
            ones been whacking off. If I find anything
            broken in there, you and I are gonna
            tangle!

An A.T.F. agent smashes the micro on the ground and sifts through the
pieces.

Nearby, Flemming and Hurley watch.

> **FLEMMING**
> (appalled)
> Masturbating in a man's camper! We're
> dealing with two sick individuals. I want
> that camper torn apart, full cavity
> searches all around.

SNAP! SFX as Agent Hurley puts on her rubber gloves and leads Tom and
Marcy away.

Agent Bork runs up to Flemming.

> **BORK**
> Chief - just came in! Two days ago,
> Express Airways had a disturbance by
> someone calling himself — Cornholio. Guess
> who matches the description?

He holds up a police sketch of Cornholio. Flemming walks to a nearby
chopper. SOUND of engine revving. Others follow.

> **FLEMMING**
> Finally, a <u>real</u> break. Get me that
> flight's point of origin. We're gonna kick
> some ass.

EXT.   DESERT - DAY

B&B walk along in the scorching heat. Ahead of them they see a
DUMB GUY and a DUMBER GUY with motorcycles parked. They are trying to
start a camp fire, LAUGHING.

> **DUMB GUY**
> (to B&B)
> Uh, hey. One of you kids got a match?

> **BUTT-HEAD**
> (dehydrated)
> Uh, my butt and your...uh, butt.

> **DUMB GUY**
> Huh huh huh huh.

INT.   B&B'S HOME - DAY

Peaceful. Empty. Suddenly dozens of A.T.F. agents break in, guns ready,
searching every corner. They tear it apart.

EXT.   B&B'S TOWN/STREETS - DAY

Agents rush down the business streets. People are in a panic. It's like
an invasion.

ANGLE ON ELITE MOTOR LODGE - ON B&B'S TV SET as agents rush by, knocking it over with a crash.

INT.   VAN DRIESSEN'S CLASS - DAY

Guitar in hand, Van Driessen sings:

> **VAN DRIESSEN**
> She flies so gracefully,
> over rocks, trees and sand. Soaring over
> cliffs and gently
> floating down to land.
> She proudly lifts her voice
> to sound her mating call.
> And soon her mate responds
> by singing..."Caw, Caw, Caw."
> Come with me, Lesbian Seagull.
> Settle down and rest with me...

Suddenly dozens of A.T.F. agents crash into the room. The door bashes in, knocking Van Driessen down hard and crushing his guitar.

Flemming enters. Behind him, McVicker.

> **McVICKER**
> Uh...uh...uh that's him. He's their
> teacher.

> **VAN DRIESSEN**
> What's going on here?

> **FLEMMING**
> I'll ask the questions. Are these your
> students?

He shows a picture of B&B.

> **VAN DRIESSEN**
> I assume you're a government agent. I
> would think you would know there's
> something in this country called due
> process.

> **FLEMMING**
> That's about the kind of talk I'd expect
> from the guy who taught these two. Take
> this scum away.

> **VAN DRIESSEN**
> I believe I'm supposed to be read my
> Miranda Rights...

An agent interrupts, punching Van Driessen in the gut. He's taken away. Flemming turns menacingly to McVicker.

> **McVICKER**
> I...I...I always knew they were no good.
> I... I... I hate them!

> **FLEMMING**
> (to McVicker)
> You've been harboring two criminal masterminds!

Bork rushes up to Flemming with a paper.

> **BORK**
> Chief, You know that guy whose camper they were whacking off in?

> **FLEMMING**
> (appalled)
> Bork! You are a federal agent. You represent the United States Government... Never end a sentence with a preposition. Try again.

> **BORK**
> Oh, ah... You know that guy in whose camper they... I mean that guy off in whose camper they were whacking?

> **FLEMMING**
> That's better. Yes?

> **BORK**
> We've run a sample through the National Criminal Sperm Bank and come up with two possible genetic matches for a father.
> (holds up photos)

TIGHT ON PHOTO. It's the DUMB GUY and DUMBER GUY from the desert.

> **BORK** (O.S./CONT.)
> Former Motley Crue roadies turned drifters.

Flemming takes the paper and marches off. Others follow.

DISSOLVE TO:

EXT. DESERT - NIGHT

B&B and the Dumb and Dumber Guys are sitting around a campfire. The Dumb Guy looks like an older, more stupid, version of Butt-Head. The Dumber Guy is a couple of evolutionary scales down from Beavis. Their relationship is an exaggerated version of B&B's.

Butt-Head is staring at the Dumb Guy in admiration. Beavis, like the Dumber Guy, appears to be just staring at the fire, hypnotized. Dumb Guy is eating spaghetti out of a can.

                    BUTT-HEAD
You were a roadie for Motley Crue?

                    DUMB GUY
                         (mouth full)
Yup. Huh huh.

                    BEAVIS
Fire.

                    DUMB GUY
Here's another true story. About fifteen
years ago, we stopped in this, uh, toilet,
called Highland...

                    BUTT-HEAD
Really? That's where we're from.

                    DUMB GUY
Well, then you know what I'm talking
about. Anyway, here's the story. I
scored with these two chicks. True story.

                    BUTT-HEAD
You scored with two chicks?!

                    DUMB GUY
                         (spaghetti dribbling from mouth)
Yeah, they were sluts. Huh huh huh.

                    DUMBER GUY
Ih hih hih hih hih hih.

Dumb Guy punches Dumber Guy in the head with a closed fist.

                    DUMB GUY
Shut up, dumb-ass! You didn't score. I
scored with both of them...

BUTT-HEAD
Uh, do you think these two sluts still
live in Highland? That would be cool.

DUMB GUY
(After taking another big bite)
Hey, you wanna see something <u>really</u> cool?
Huh huh huh.

Dumb Guy gets up, turns his butt towards the fire and starts to drop his
pants.

EXT.   DESERT/LONG SHOT - CONTINUOUS

The campfire is in the distance, middle of nowhere. A flatulant sound
is heard. Suddenly, a big beautiful purple and orange fireball erupts,
lighting up the sky.

B&B/DUMB GUY/DUMBER GUY (O.S.)
Huh huh huh huh huh huh huh huh huh huh

BEAVIS (O.S.)
Fire.

EXT.   DESERT - MORNING

B&B wake up. The Dumb Guy and Dumber Guy are gone. The sun is
scorching.

B&B inch forward - spent, dehydrated, near death.

ANGLE ON GROUND as B&B collapse into frame. Butt-Head looks up at the
sun, squinting.

BUTT-HEAD
(barely alive)
The sun sucks.

A vulture picks at Beavis' shirt. Beavis SMACKS the vulture.

BEAVIS
(to the vulture)
Cut it out butt-hole!

The vulture moves revealing a PEYOTE CACTUS. Beavis looks at it.

BEAVIS (CONT.)
Hey Butt-Head, isn't there supposed to be
like, water in cactuses?

BUTT-HEAD
(semiconscious)
Uh...

60

Beavis takes a bite of the cactus, chews and then coughs.

>   **BUTT-HEAD** (CONT.)
>   (sees something)
>   Hey Beavis, check it out.

IN FRONT OF B&B: Two vultures start humping.

>   **B&B**
>   (struggling to laugh)
>   Huh huh huh (cough) huh huh (cough).

EXT.   ROADBLOCK - DAY

START ON SUN - over B&B?

REVEAL it's over Muddy who looks at a picture of B&B held by an A.T.F. agent.

>   **MUDDY**
>   No, I can't say I've seen 'em. I sure hope
>   it's safe to drive around here.

>   **COP**
>   Don't worry, sir. Just stick to the main
>   roads. If they're around, they're probably
>   hiding out in the desert.

>   **MUDDY**
>   That's good to know, Officer.

Muddy takes off with a smile and turns off onto a side road.

EXT. DESERT - LATER

B&B barely crawling forward. Butt-Head stops, then Beavis. They're barely able to talk.

>   **BEAVIS**
>   Hey Butt-Head, are we gonna die?

>   **BUTT-HEAD**
>   Uh, probably, huh huh...Whoa, I think my
>   life is like, flashing in front of my
>   eyes!

BUTT-HEAD'S VISION. Through time-lapse dissolves we see him sitting on his couch with Beavis, laughing like an idiot in the exact same positions at age 2, 5, 7, 10, 13.

>   **BUTT-HEAD**
>   Whoa, my life is cool!

TIGHT ON BEAVIS:

> **BEAVIS**
> Uh... I think I'm seeing something too.
> It's like a really long time ago...

BEAVIS' VISION: Beavis as a sperm cell swimming through a uterus. It's a sperm cell with the face of Beavis on it.

> **BEAVIS/SPERM**
> Yeah, heh heh. This is gonna be cool.

Beavis/sperm swims over to the egg.

With it's own tail the Beavis/Sperm starts picking it's nose.

> **BEAVIS/SPERM** (CONT.)
> Hey, how's it goin'? Heh heh heh.

Several other sperm charge in knocking Beavis into the egg. His conception looks like a dumb accident.

BACK ON BEAVIS:

> **BEAVIS**
> Yeah, heh heh I scored.

Animated bubbles appear around Beavis' head.

> **BEAVIS** (CONT.)
> Hey Butt-Head, I'm starting to feel weird.
> I think I'm freaking out.

> **BUTT-HEAD**
> Huh? huh huh.

> **BEAVIS**
> Whoa, this is cool! Heh heh. It's like,
> everything looks all weird and...

BEAVIS' P.O.V. OF BUTT-HEAD: His face starts to warp and colors start shifting.

> **BEAVIS** (CONT.)
> ...and... Whoa!...and it's like there's
> all these weird shapes and it's sort of
> like,...it's like...like a MUSIC VIDEO!!!

Tight on Beavis' face staring in wonder.

THIS IS WHERE THE MUSIC VIDEO/HALLUCINATION SEQUENCE BEGINS. It could even be so shameless as to actually have a chyron in the lower left hand corner.

I would like to have a band (White Zombie?) do a version of something like, "Fire," by The Crazy World of Arthur Brown. This is the song that begins, "I am God of Hellfire and I bring you...fire!"

The concept of this will depend somewhat on which band we get, but I would like to see it get pretty wild and surreal. (If it's White Zombie, we could incorporate some of Rob Zombies artwork.)

BEAVIS' P.O.V.:

We see the sun above the horizon turn into a giant ball of fire. The ball of fire develops a face and speaks.

                    FIRE
          I am God of Hellfire and I bring
          you...(music begins) Fire...

                    BEAVIS
          Whoa!!! This kicks ass!!!

THIS IS THE GREATEST VIDEO BEAVIS HAS EVER SEEN. Out of the ball of fire steps a beautiful woman in a bikini.

At first the video is mostly the God of Hellfire, chicks in bikini's and various images of B&B's TV in all it's glory.

As the video/hallucination continues, it becomes a psychotic mass of naked people, fire, TVs, vultures, B&B head-banging, weird stuff from my high school notebooks, etc.

At one point we see the God of Hellfire in a Burger World uniform.

As the song winds down, we incorporate Muddy's car into the surreal imagery. (We should also incorporate their TV, as well as maybe some of the characters from the show that aren't in the movie.)

Then, we REVEAL Muddy's car actually pulling up to B&B's near-dead bodies.

The SONG ENDS as Muddy tosses water on B&B. REVEAL they were not far from the side of a road all along.

                    B&B
          Ahhhhghhhhgh!

B&B snap out of it. They rise and find Muddy hovering over them with a shotgun.

>   **BEAVIS**
>   Aagh! I'm all wet!...(realizing) Oh, cool.
>   Heh heh heh. Water.

Muddy aims his shotgun at B&B.

>   **MUDDY**
>   Ah'm gonna enjoy this. Any last words
>   b'fore ah kill ya?

B&B think.

>   **BUTT-HEAD**
>   Uh.... Huh huh. I have a couple. Butt
>   cheeks, huh huh huh.

>   **BEAVIS**
>   Yeah! Boobs. Heh heh. I just wanna say
>   that again. Boobs. Heh heh.

>   **MUDDY**
>   Ah'm gonna blow you both to hell!

>   **BUTT-HEAD**
>   Cool, huh huh. (realizing) Hey Beavis
>   that's that dude that's paying us to do
>   his wife.

>   **BEAVIS**
>   Oh yeah. Can you just take us to
>   Washington. We're gonna meet her there
>   and, you know, heh heh hmmm...

>   **MUDDY**
>   Washington! That's where she was gonna
>   meet up with ya? (realizes) Damn, she's
>   goin' all the way!

>   **B&B**
>   Huh huh huh huh huh huh huh.

Muddy lowers the gun a bit.

>   **MUDDY**
>   You know, I just might need you after all.
>   Aw right, in the trunk. You're gonna help
>   me get mah *unit* back.

Muddy pops it open. B&B climb in. Muddy closes the trunk on them and
walks to the front of the car. HOLD ON THE TRUNK.

>   **BUTT-HEAD** (O.S.)
>   Boy, it sure is hard to score. Huh huh
>   huh.

Muddy peels out.

EXT.   HIGHWAY - DAY

A MONTAGE SONG BEGINS.

Muddy drives by.

INSERT: A RED LINE snakes through a map to Santa Fe.

DISSOLVE TO:

EXT.   HIGHWAY - DAY

Muddy's car drives by. Muddy hears B&B laugh from inside the trunk and turns up the radio to drown it out.

INSERT: A RED LINE snakes through a map to Oklahoma City.

DISSOLVE TO:

EXT.   GAS STATION - DAY

Muddy pumps gas. From inside the trunk:

> **BEAVIS** (O.C.)
> Hey Butt-Head, look. A jack. Heh heh.

> **BUTT-HEAD** (O.C.)
> Huh huh. Jack. Huh huh.

INSERT: A RED LINE snakes through a map to Little Rock, Nashville and into Virginia up Rt. 81.

EXT. MUDDY'S CAR DRIVING ON HIGHWAY - DAY

ANGLE OUTSIDE MUDDY'S TRUNK. From within we hear:

> **BUTT-HEAD** (O.C.)
> Hey, Beavis, check it out. I'm jacking
> off!

> **B&B**
> Huh huh huh huh huh huh.

Pumping up the jack, they cause the lid of the trunk to start to bend.

Suddenly, it pops open. B&B are a sweaty mess. They gasp.

> **BUTT-HEAD**
> This sucks. Let's get outta here.

They look out. The road behind them races past at 80mph. Beavis
stares dumbly.

> **BEAVIS**
> Uh, you first.

> **BUTT-HEAD**
> C'mon, Beavis, just start running really
> fast when you hit the ground. It'll work.

> **BEAVIS**
> Okay. I'll go right after you.

Butt-Head shoves Beavis out of the car.

> **BEAVIS** (CONT.)
> Ahhhhghghhghghgh!

Beavis tries to run, but hits the road and flips over and over - and
smashes his butt.

> **BEAVIS** (CONT.)
> Owwwwww, my butt!!!!!!

His body stops in the middle of the road. A huge truck, about to hit
him, swerves and jackknifes over the side.

Behind the truck, several cars screech to a halt, one smashing into the
other.

ANGLE ON MUDDY'S TRUNK.

Butt-Head looks at the road.

> **BUTT-HEAD**
> Huh huh huh huh huh. That was cool.

ANGLE ON MUDDY'S TIRE. It hits a pothole.

ANGLE ON BUTT-HEAD, shooting out of the trunk, he grabs onto the lid. He
bounces against the road again and again.

Finally, he loses his grip as the lid to the trunk closes.

ANGLE ON BUTT-HEAD, rolling along the highway.

A car, about to hit Butt-Head, screeches to a halt. Other cars behind it
smash and pile up.

ANGLE ON ROAD SOME WAYS BACK. On Tom and Marcy in their car.

                              TOM
                    Boy, what I wouldn't give for five minutes
                    alone with them two little bastards...

The car ahead of Tom crashes into the car ahead of that. Tom crashes
into it. And the car behind crashes into Tom.

OVERHEAD ANGLE shows cars and trucks behind, crashing, piling up. A
massive pile-up.

INT.   MUDDY'S CAR - DAY

Muddy doesn't notice the mess behind him. He drives on.

MONTAGE SONG ENDS

EXT.   HIGHWAY - DAY

LATER.

ON MEDIVAC helicopters; one landing, another taking off.

MOVE TO WOMAN TV REPORTER, talking to camera:

                            REPORTER
                    Authorities are calling this the worst
                    highway disaster in the nation's
                    history...

INT.   A.T.F. HEADQUARTERS/FLEMMING'S OFFICE - DAY

Flemming, Bork, and about six other agents look at a map. Behind them, a
TV is on with the reporter continuing. Behind the reporter, B&B poke
their heads into frame at 45 degree angles, looking like deer in the
headlights.

                        REPORTER (Cont.)
                    ... Behind me, over 400 vehicles lay
                    wrecked or stuck. No one knows what caused
                    it, but police have not ruled out the
                    possibility of terrorists.

Bork notices B&B on TV and taps Flemming on the shoulder. Flemming
looks.

                          FLEMMING
                    Well, I'll be a blue-nosed gopher.

                            BORK
                        (despairing)
                    Where did these guys come from?

Flemming looks at the big map which traces sightings of B&B across America.

> **FLEMMING**
> The question is, where are they going.

He looks again at the TV. On the news, a story about...

> **REPORTER 2**
> ...set for 5:00 tomorrow when representatives from around the world will meet in Washington for the first such peace conference...

Flemming back at the map, and then back at the TV.

> **FLEMMING**
> What the hell...? Bork! That bus we picked up. Where was it headin'?

> **BORK**
> (checks papers)
> D.C., Chief.

> **FLEMMING**
> (realizing)
> Jesus jumped-up... Bork, can you imagine what would happen if they set that thing off in our nation's capitol, or even worse, if they sold it to some damned foreigner at that conference. (rises and puts his fist down) Well, it's not gonna happen!

EXT. HIGHWAY/CRASH SIGHT - DAY

B&B walk along looking at the wreckage.

> **BUTT-HEAD**
> Whoa, this kicks ass! Huh huh huh.

> **MARTHA** (O.S.)
> Yoo-hoo! Travis and Bob Head. Whoo-hoo!

The tour bus stands nearby. Martha calls from the window.

> **BEAVIS**
> Hey Butt-Head it's that chick!

> **BUTT-HEAD**
> Uh, oh yeah. Cool. They can take us to Washington and we can finally score.

B&B head into the bus.

> **BEAVIS**
> Yeah, heh heh. Umm, isn't Seattle in
> Washington? Heh heh.... 'cuz I was
> thinking maybe we could go see Hole.

> **BUTT-HEAD**
> Yeah. We can go see Hole and then we can
> get some hole. Huh huh huh huh.

INSERT: MAP. The RED LINE snakes right up to D.C.

INT/EXT.   TOUR BUS - DAY

INTERCUT BETWEEN THE BUS AND THE SIGHTS IT PASSES:

ANGLE ON THE LINCOLN MONUMENT.

ANGLE ON BUS WINDOW. Several seniors press their faces to see.

ANGLE ON THE WASHINGTON MONUMENT.

ANGLE ON BUS WINDOW. More seniors rush to the window to see.

ANGLE ON THE CAPITOL BUILDING.

ANGLE ON BUS WINDOW. B&B press their bare asses.

EXT. CAPITOL - DAY

The seniors and B&B get off the bus.

As soon as they're out of sight, Dallas drives up and sees the Tour Bus.
She smiles to herself.

INT.   CAPITOL UNDERGROUND GARAGE - DAY

Dark. Isolated.

Dallas pulls up and gets out of her car. Suddenly, a voice:

> **VOICE/MUDDY**
> 'Spectin' someone?

Dallas wheels around. Muddy's got a gun on her.

> **MUDDY** (CONT.)
> Well, well. Look at this. The love of my
> life. Where <u>have</u> you been?

Muddy moves towards Dallas. She steps back.

69

                         DALLAS
              Honey, I was gonna split it with you after
              I sold it, right down the middle. I swear.
              I just...

                         MUDDY
              Sure you were. But now you don't have to
              go through all that bother.

Dallas moves seductively towards Muddy.

                         DALLAS
              Come on Muddy. Whatd' ya say we just
              forget about it and go get a room like old
              times...

Muddy cocks his gun.

                         MUDDY
              I don't think so. Where is it?

INT.   CAPITOL - DAY

B&B walk up to the information booth where a HOST makes an announcement.

                         HOST
                      (announces)
              All Senators are requested for a vote. All
              Senators are requested for a vote.

A bell accompanies the announcement.

                         HOST (CONT.)
                      (to B&B)
              Can I help you?

                         BEAVIS
              Yeah, we're looking for Washington.

                         BUTT-HEAD
              Huh huh. We're gonna meet this chick with
              really big hooters.

                         HOST
              Sirs, you are in Washington.

                         BEAVIS
              Well where is she?!

                         BUTT-HEAD
              Could you, like, tell her we're ready to
              score?

                           70

                              HOST
                     No! Just a moment...

She turns to the side to answer the phone.

INT.   CAPITOL/PRIVATE PANEL ROOM - DAY

Six Senators sit behind a panel. BOB PACKWOOD testifies across from
them.

                            SENATOR
                     Thank you for returning, Senator Packwood,
                     to help us understand how sexual
                     harassment happens in this sacred
                     institution.

Suddenly, SOUND OF BEAVIS over the PA.

                        BUTT-HEAD (V.O.)
                     Uh... Attention, attention! We're looking
                     for that chick with the big boobs.

                          BEAVIS (V.O.)
                     Heh heh. We wanna do her now!

                           HOST (V.O.)
                     Hey! Gimme tha...

                           B&B (V.O.)
                     Huh huh huh huh huh.

ANGLE ON PACKWOOD - smiles.

                           PACKWOOD
                     Huh huh huh huh huh.

INT.   CAPITOL/SENATE - DAY

Classic wide, overhead shot. SOUND of all Senators.

                           SENATORS
                     Huh huh huh huh huh.

INT.   CAPITOL UNDERGROUND GARAGE - DAY

Muddy finishes tying Dallas' hands behind her back. He crosses to his
trunk.

                            MUDDY
                     You forgot who yer dealin' with, Honey. Ya
                     see, I got your mules right here in my
                     trunk and...

Muddy pops the trunk. It's empty.

> **MUDDY** (CONT.)
> Say what?... I'm gonna kill 'em!!!

> **DALLAS**
> No honey <u>we're</u> gonna kill 'em.

Dallas, still tied up, starts kissing Muddy. He gives in.

EXT.   CAPITOL - DAY

ANGLE ON B&B getting on the bus last.

INT. TOUR BUS - DAY

Butt-Head sits. Beavis pauses, still standing.

> **BEAVIS**
> Hey wait a minute. What's going on? Why
> are we getting back on the bus?

> **OLD GUY**
> It's time to go son.

> **BEAVIS**
> We can't leave! We never met that chick!
> Dammit!!! We were supposed to get some!

> **BUTT-HEAD**
> Huh huh huh. Settle down Beavis.

> **BEAVIS**
> Oh yeah,...I mean no. NO! I won't settle
> down! Not this time!...

Beavis is shaking, fed up. He delivers the speech of his life.

> **BEAVIS** (CONT.)
> Dammit, this always happens! I think I'm
> gonna score and then I never score! It's
> not fair! We've traveled a hundred miles
> 'cause we thought we were gonna score, but
> now it's not gonna happen!

> **BUS DRIVER**
> (yelling from his seat)
> Hey buddy, sit down! Now!

BEAVIS
SHUT UP! (continuing) I'm sick and tired
of this! We're never gonna score! It's
just not gonna happen! We're just gonna
get old like these people, but they've
probably scored!

BUS DRIVER
(standing)
Hey! I'm warning you! Sit down!

BEAVIS
It's like this chick's a slut (motioning
to Martha)... and look at this guy!...
He's old but he's probably scored a
million times!

OLD GUY
(nods in agreement)
Ohh yeah.

BEAVIS
But not us! We're never gonna score! WE'RE
NEVER GONNA SCORE!!! AAGGHHHH!!!

The bus driver tackles Beavis.

INT. CAPITOL/PARKING GARAGE/MUDDY'S CAR - DAY

In a tight shot, we see Muddy and Dallas humping away in the back seat
(in a PG-13 kind of way).

We hear the sound of a door opening.

ANGLE ON FLEMMING, BORK AND SEVERAL AGENTS LOOKING DOWN.

FLEMMING
Well look what we have here. You two make
me sick... Book 'em Bork.

DALLAS
You don't have anything on us and you know
it.

FLEMMING
Oh I don't huh? How about lewd conduct?
Maybe indecent exposure?...
Here's what's gonna happen. One of you's
gonna make a deal and get me the *unit*. The
other can spend the next sixty years in
jail.

                              MUDDY
                There you're wrong, boy. Me and mah wife
                are back together and you'll never...

                              DALLAS
                <u>He</u> stole the *unit*. Said he put it in some
                kid's pants.

                              MUDDY
                Why you damn little...

He's cuffed and dragged away.

INT.   TOUR BUS - DAY

The driver sits down and drives on.

Beavis is slightly beat up. Martha reaches into her purse, filled with
prescription medications.

                              MARTHA
                Now Travis, it doesn't do a body good to
                get all worked up. Here. This should help
                you relax.

She holds up a box of NoDrowz and squints at the label.

                              MARTHA
                Does that say Xanax?

                              BEAVIS
                Um, um, yeah, probably. Heh heh.

Beavis takes a couple, then starts wolfing down the whole box.

INT.   FLEMMING'S CAR - DAY

Flemming's on the radio. Bork checks a tour guide.

                              FLEMMING
                      (to radio)
                Okay, boys and girls, our suspects are on
                a tour bus we believe to be heading for...
                (checks papers) the White House! Jumpin'
                Jesus! I want everyone there. Our people.
                Locals. Orders are shoot to kill. Repeat!
                Shoot to kill!

                              BORK
                Chief, I swear, we tore that bus apart.
                They couldn't have...

74

                              FLEMMING
                    Bork, when this is all over, remind me to
                    make you an appointment with Agent Hurley.

EXT.   STREETS OF WASHINGTON - DAY

All manner of police, A.T.F., F.B.I. cars speed along.

EXT.   WHITE HOUSE/TOURIST PARKING LOT - DAY

B&B and the seniors walk from the bus to the White House. Beavis is
starting to shake as he finishes off the NoDrowz.

NEARBY, Anderson's Camper pulls up.

INT.   WHITE HOUSE - DAY

The seniors and B&B are being led on a tour. B&B in back. Beavis is
starting to SHAKE AND MAKE STRANGE NOISES.

As the tour moves on, Beavis stays behind. He goes over to a coffee-
serving cart sitting outside a meeting room. He starts WOLFING DOWN
SUGAR CUBES.

BACK ON THE TOUR:

The tour is led by a smiling guide, SANDY.

                              SANDY
                    Welcome to the White House. My name is
                    Sandy, and I'll be your tour guide. In
                    case you don't know it, you've come on a
                    very special day. Today...

She points to the camera crews outside the window.

EXT.   WHITE HOUSE LAWN - DAY

ON A NEWS REPORTER, facing camera. Behind her, a large gathering before
a stage.

                              REPORTER
                    Today, representatives from around the
                    world are gathered at the White House for
                    an historic global conference called: Give
                    Peace A Chance - or G-PAC.

EXT.   WHITE HOUSE ENTRANCE - DAY

A.T.F., Police and F.B.I. cars arrive.

INT.   WHITE HOUSE TOUR - DAY

The tour stands in the East Room.

> **SANDY**
> This is the East Room. Many of the portraits you see were saved from the fire set by the British in 1814...

Beavis is shaking, babbling, staring at his fist, etc.

> **BEAVIS**
> Heh heh. Fire. Heh heh Aaaaeeehhhhg!!!

> **BUTT-HEAD**
> What's your problem Beavis?

> **SANDY**
> ...The site for the White House was chosen by President Washington and Pierre L'Enfant...

Beavis now has his T-shirt pulled over his head and is pacing around and babbling. He's too loud now for Sandy to ignore.

> **BEAVIS**
> L'enfentatta tiitatta for my bunghole!

> **SANDY**
> Sir, are you okay?

> **BEAVIS**
> Are you threatening me?! I am Cornholio!

> **SANDY**
> Sir, maybe you should wait out in the lobby.

Beavis/Cornholio wanders off, muttering.

> **BEAVIS/CORNHOLIO**
> In thees lobby, wheel there be T.P.?

EXT.   WHITE HOUSE - DAY

ON FLEMMING AND THE HEAD SECRET SERVICE GUY - arguing.

> **FLEMMING**
> You don't understand. National security is at stake here. We <u>must</u> evacuate.

> **SECRET SERVICE GUY**
> Not without proper authorization.

INT. WHITE HOUSE - DAY

A group of foreign dignitaries is being led through the hallway on a tour. Two of them chat in Spanish.

We see Beavis coming down the hall in the opposite direction.

> **DIGNITARY #1**
> El Presidente es un gringo muy gordo, no?

> **DIGNITARY #2**
> Si.

They pass Beavis Babbling — riffing off their Spanish.

> **BEAVIS/CORNHOLIO**
> Gr-r-ringo! Burrito! R-r-anddatattta!!

Beavis turns around and stops.

> **BEAVIS/CORNHOLIO** (CONT.)
> I am Cornholio! I need T.P. for my bunghole! Heh heh heh.

The group continues down the hall, ignoring Beavis.

> **BEAVIS/CORNHOLIO** (CONT.)
> (humble)
> Would you like to *see* my bunghole?

Beavis leaves.

INT. WHITE HOUSE/CORRIDOR OF PRESIDENTS - DAY

Tom and Marcy Anderson gaze at a portrait of Eisenhower.

> **TOM**
> (sotto)
> Where are ya when we need ya Ike... (to Marcy) I tell ya what, Honey, with all we been through, it don't change a thing. I said it before and I'll say it again. This is the greatest country on earth...

Beavis/Cornholio wanders by behind them. Tom turns to look.

TOM'S BLURRY P.O.V.: We see Beavis/Cornholio wander down the hall BABBLING.

> **TOM**
> (adjusting his glasses)
> Say, that looks like... Nah, it couldn't be.

INT. WHITE HOUSE/ANOTHER PART OF THE HALLWAY - DAY

Beavis comes around a corner and stops at a portrait of Nixon.

ANGLE ON PORTRAIT. Nixon doing classic victory pose - peace signs with both hands up.

ANGLE ON BEAVIS. His hands also up in the Cornholio pose. He stares for a beat, then:

> **BEAVIS/CORNHOLIO**
> Are you threatening me?!... I am
> Cornholio!

Beavis wanders off.

INT. PRESS ROOM - DAY

The press secretary is giving a conference. The room is packed with reporters.

> **PRESS SECRETARY**
> Yes, the president does plan to speak
> today at the G-PAC conference.

> **REPORTERS**
> (raising hands)
> Mr. Secretary! Mr. Secretary! What about
> the rumors that a biological weapon has
> been stolen and smuggled out of the
> country at this conference. Mr. Secretary!

> **SECRETARY**
> Those rumors are entirely unfounded....

While this goes on: Through a doorway in the back of the room, we see Beavis wander out of frame and then come back in.

He starts WOLFING DOWN MORE SUGAR CUBES from a coffee serving cart.

> **BEAVIS**
> I am the great Cornholio. I am a gringo...

EXT. WHITE HOUSE - DAY

IN MONTAGE SHOTS:

A.T.F. and Secret Service agents argue.

Several S.W.A.T. trucks pull up.

S.W.A.T. team guys jump out of trucks and load guns.

INT.   WHITE HOUSE TOUR - DAY

The tour stands in a giant, elegant dining room.

                    SANDY
          This is the State Dining Room where the
          most powerful world leaders are
          entertained.

                    BUTT-HEAD
          Uh, where's the TV? Huh huh huh. Hey
          Beavis,... Beavis?

Butt-Head wanders off.

                    BUTT-HEAD (CONT.)
          This house sucks.

INT. HALLWAY OUTSIDE OF OVAL OFFICE - DAY

A Secret Service guard is talking on radio/phone.

                    GUARD
          Evacuation?... Probably just another bomb
          threat or something... OK.

The guard walks off down the hallway, leaving his post.

From the other end of the hallway we see Beavis/Cornholio enter, still
babbling.

INT.   WHITE HOUSE/OVAL OFFICE - DAY

Beavis wanders in and finds no one around. He shouts in frustration.

                    BEAVIS/CORNHOLIO
          I am the great Cornholio! Heh heh. You
          will cooperate with my bunghole!

He picks up the *red phone* and presses the button again and again.

INT.   STRATEGIC AIR COMMAND - DAY

The war room. A LIEUTENANT picks up the *red phone*.

A TITLE COMES UP: STRATEGIC AIR COMMAND.

                    LIEUTENANT
          Yes, Mr. President.

BEAVIS/CORNHOLIO
(on phone)
I am Meester President! I have no
bunghole! I am Cornholio!

LIEUTENANT
Mr. President, I can't make out what
you're saying.

BEAVIS/CORNHOLIO
(on phone)
Bungholio! Presidente! I need teepee!

A GENERAL comes by.

LIEUTENANT
(to general)
Sir, the President sounds strange.
Something's going on. I don't think it's a
drill.

GENERAL
Washington may be under attack. Go to
Defcon 4.

ANGLE ON THE LIEUTENANT'S HAND, moving to push a button. Alarms sound.

ANGLE ON BIG MAP. A sign flashes: DEFCON 4. Soldiers run through frame.

EXT. WHITE HOUSE - DAY

The seniors, along with other tourists and dignitaries are escorted out
of the building.

INT.   WHITE HOUSE CORRIDOR - DAY

A.T.F. agents rush by. We HOLD here after they go. Butt-Head walks by,
unaware.

Butt-Head walks around and opens a door. The door to CHELSEA CLINTON'S
room.

Inside, she's folding clothes. (NOTE: If Clinton is not reelected, the
shot will be wider, revealing she's packing a suitcase)

BUTT-HEAD
(excited)
Whoa! Huh huh uh,... (suave) Hey, baby.
Huh huh, I noticed you have braces. So do
I, huh huh.

80

EXT. WHITE HOUSE - DAY

We HOLD ON A WIDE SHOT of the back of the White House for a beat. Then:

We see Butt-Head come CRASHING out of a second-story window - thrown by Chelsea. He lands deep in the bushes below.

ANGLE ON the bushes.

                         BUTT-HEAD
              Huh huh huh. That was cool.

We see Butt-Head slowly emerge from the bushes. He looks up, suddenly seeing:

DOZENS OF A.T.F. AGENTS surround him, rifles trained.

                    BUTT-HEAD (CONT.)
                       (awestruck)
              This is the coolest thing I have ever
              seen.

Flemming steps up.

                         FLEMMING
              Alright, where's the *unit*?

                         BUTT-HEAD
              Uh, in my pants?

Bork and others quickly frisk Butt-Head.

                         BORK
              Not on him, Chief.

                         FLEMMING
              Agent Hurley...

Hurley steps forward.

                    FLEMMING (CONT.)
              ... I want you to give this scum bag a
              cavity search. I'm talkin' Roto-Rooter.
              Don't stop 'till you reach the back of his
              teeth.

Butt-Head is led away.

INT.   OVAL OFFICE - DAY

Beavis is on the *red phone*. He goes through the President's drawers.

                        LIEUTENANT
                        (on phone)
            Mr. President, the bombers are scrambled.
            Sir, we're awaiting your final orders.

                     BEAVIS/CORNHOLIO
            I order you to surrender your T.P.!

INT.   STRATEGIC AIR COMMAND - DAY

The General grabs the phone from the Lieutenant.

                        GENERAL
            Gimme that! (to phone) Mr. President, in
            the name of all that is holy, I must have
            those launch codes!

                        BEAVIS
                        (on phone)
            Are you threatening me? Bungholio!

Click. Beavis hangs up.

INT.   WHITE HOUSE/OVAL OFFICE - DAY

Beavis walks out of the Oval Office.

                     BEAVIS/CORNHOLIO
            Presidente bungholio! You will cooperate
            with my bunghole!

INT. A.T.F. VAN - DAY

Hurley steps out of a van to speak with Flemming and Bork. She pulls off
a LONG GLOVE that goes almost to her shoulder.

Butt-Head sits, disheveled.

                        BUTT-HEAD
            Uh, huh huh, did I just score?

                        HURLEY
            He's clean, chief.

                        FLEMMING
            The other guy must have it. He's gotta be
            in here somewhere.(re: Butt-Head) Bring
            him.

Flemming, Bork and the other agents take off.

INT. WHITE HOUSE - DAY

In the main reception area, Beavis is surrounded by a few FOREIGN
DIGNITARIES who try to make sense of what he is saying.

> DIGNITARY #1
> Que es un "bunghole"? Que lengua es?
> Arabigo?

> DIGNITARY #2
> De donde eres tu?

> BEAVIS/CORNHOLIO
> Arabigo? I am the Great Cornholio. I have
> no bunghole. Where I come from there is no
> T.P.

A White House representative comes up. He assumes Beavis is with the
dignitaries.

> REPRESENTATIVE
> I'm terribly sorry for the inconvenience
> gentlemen, but we're going to have to wait
> outside for a moment. Follow me please.

He leads them out, including Beavis who continues to babble.

> BEAVIS/CORNHOLIO
> You can run but you cannot hide from the
> Almighty Bunghole! Heh heh hmm.

EXT. WHITE HOUSE - DAY

Beavis/Cornholio and the dignitaries are escorted out. Beavis,
unnoticed, keeps walking.

Beavis, walking along stops. He sees something.

> BEAVIS/CORNHOLIO
> Aaaaahh...

ON BEAVIS' P.O.V. across the street, we see what Beavis is looking at:

ANDERSON'S CAMPER.

ANGLE ON BEAVIS. He takes the picture of Dallas out of his pocket.

TIGHT ON the picture of Dallas.

TIGHT ON Anderson's camper.

TIGHT ON Beavis.

BEAVIS/CORNHOLIO (CONT.)

> Aaaahh, heh heh...

Beavis looks alternately at the camper and the picture a couple of times, and then walks across the street.

BEAVIS/CORNHOLIO (CONT.)

> Booiiing! Ptang ptang! Wagh-hah!!!

Beavis goes into Anderson's camper and shuts the door.

A Secret Service agent walks by, just missing Beavis.

INT. WHITE HOUSE/CORRIDOR OF PRESIDENTS - DAY

Tom and Marcy enjoying a moment.

TOM

> Boy I tell ya what, it really makes ya
> proud. I could stay here all day.

An A.T.F. agent comes up and interrupts Tom.

AGENT

> Sir, I'm gonna have to ask you to leave...

TOM

> Now wait just a minute...

AGENT

> Now!

NEARBY, Flemming and Bork are showing the police sketch of Cornholio to Sandy and questioning her.

Bork sees Anderson walk by from a distance.

BORK

> Say chief, isn't that the guy whose
> camper,...I mean, off in whose...

FLEMMING

> (irritated)
> Not now Bork.

EXT. ANDERSON'S CAMPER - DAY

From inside the camper we hear THE STRANGEST CORNHOLIO SOUNDS YET.

ANGLE ON the front of the camper. Tom and Marcy walk up.

> **TOM**
> I tell ya what honey, this country's goin'
> to Hell in a handbasket.

They get in the front. Tom adjusts the side-view mirror.

> **TOM** (CONT.)
> I'm gonna go over right now and talk to my
> Congressman about this...

TOM'S P.O.V.. In the side-view mirror we see the camper SHAKING and hear
Beavis/Cornholio.

> **BEAVIS/CORNHOLIO** (O.S.)
> Ooooaaaaaghhh!!! Whack-awhack-aaaaghh!!!

> **TOM**
> What the hell?...Wait here a minute...

Tom gets out and goes into the camper.

HOLD ON THE CAMPER DOOR.

Tom throws Beavis/Cornholio out the door. Beavis is in his underwear
with his T-shirt still pulled over his head.

> **TOM** (CONT.)
> And if I ever catch ya whackin' in here
> again I'm gonna hog-tie ya! (to himself)
> Now I gotta straighten up in here.

Tom goes back in the camper.

> **BEAVIS/CORNHOLIO**
> You have offended my bunghole!

EXT. WHITE HOUSE - DAY

Bork reports to Flemming. Butt-Head is held by two agents.

> **BORK**
> We just cleared all four floors. No sign
> of him.

> **FLEMMING**
> Damn! Where the hell is he? We should've
> found him by now.

Bork sees something. It's Beavis, about a hundred yards away.

> **BORK**
> Chief, look!

               FLEMMING
               (picks up radio)
     Attention all units. We've got him. He's
     in front of a camper in the visitor's lot.

EXT. OUTSIDE ANDERSON'S CAMPER - DAY

Beavis stands, T-shirt still over his head. Suddenly, dozens of agents
surround him, pointing guns at him. Beavis seems oblivious to the
danger.

             BEAVIS/CORNHOLIO
     I am the great Cornholio! I will lay waste
     to your bunghole! Heh heh.

BEHIND THE AGENTS, Flemming approaches and gives orders.

               FLEMMING
     OK, nobody shoot. He could still have the
     unit on him. Keep your distance. We don't
     wanna take a chance on hitting it.

               BORK
     Where are his pants?

               FLEMMING
     Who knows...

Beavis reaches to scratch his butt. Agents step back, cautious.

Flemming picks up a bullhorn and addresses Beavis.

             FLEMMING (CONT.)
               (on bullhorn)
     This is Agent Flemming, A.T.F.. We won't
     hurt you. We just want the unit. Tell us
     where the unit is.

             BEAVIS/CORNHOLIO
     Do you have T.P.? T.P. for my bunghole?

               FLEMMING
               (on bullhorn)
     We'll get you whatever you want. (to
     agents) Get that other kid. We might need
     him.

             BEAVIS/CORNHOLIO
     Do you have any oleo? Heh heh.

BORK
(on a radio)
This is Bork. We need some T.P. and
some...(to Flemming) What'd he say?

ANGLE BEHIND AGENTS. Butt-Head is brought in by two agents.

BUTT-HEAD
Whoa, this rules! Can I have a gun too?
Huh huh huh.

ON BEAVIS. He continues to babble, making the agents nervous.

BEAVIS/CORNHOLIO
You must bow down to the Almighty
Bunghole. (Beavis) Heh heh, this is cool.
(Cornholio, chanting) Bungholio-o-o-o-o-o!

FLEMMING
(to Bork)
He's jerkin' us off. I Think we're gonna
have to take him out. Get ready to fire on
my orders... (on bullhorn) This is your
last chance. Give us the
unit now...

BEAVIS/CORNHOLIO
(Beavis) Why does everyone wanna see my
schlong? (Cornholio, chanting) I am the
one-and-only-almighty-bungholiooo!

FLEMMING:
(to agents)
OK boys. Get ready to fire on the count of
three. (on bullhorn) I'm gonna give you
three seconds...

ANGLE ON AGENTS taking aim, cocking their guns.

FLEMMING (CONT.)
(on bullhorn)
One...

ANGLE ON BEAVIS, chanting.

BEAVIS/CORNHOLIO
Cornholio-o-o-o-o...

ANGLE ON BUTT-HEAD.

BUTT-HEAD
Uh, huh huh huh.

                              FLEMMING
                          (on bullhorn)
                ...Two...

                          BEAVIS/CORNHOLIO
          ...o-o-o-eieee-ooooeeeooooo...

                              FLEMMING
                          (on bullhorn)
                Thrr...

Suddenly Tom Anderson throws open his camper door, holding Beavis'
pants.

                              TOM
                And take yer damn pants with ya...!
                (noticing) What in the hell...?

                              BORK
                          (pointing)
                THE PANTS!!! He's got the unit!

Suddenly all guns are on Anderson.

                              FLEMMING
                          (through bullhorn)
                Drop the pants! Now!

                              TOM
                Wait a minute. I ain't the one...

IN SLOW MOTION:

A S.W.A.T TEAM GUY lunges at Tom, grabbing the pants.

Tom pulls away causing the pants to RIP. THE UNIT GOES FLYING.

A FROZEN MOMENT. SLOW MOTION.

TIGHT ON THE *UNIT*.

TIGHT ON FACES IN THE CROWD.

TIGHT ON THE *UNIT*.

TIGHT ON FLEMMING.

TIGHT ON BUTT-HEAD, LAUGHING IN SLOW MOTION - OBLIVIOUS.

TIGHT ON THE *UNIT*, FALLING, FALLING.

IT HIT'S BUTT-HEAD'S HEAD, BOUNCES AND FALLS INTO HIS HANDS.

                                88

The agents all stare at Butt-Head - quiet, not sure what to do.

Butt-Head hands it to Flemming, nonchalant.

> **BUTT-HEAD**
> Uh, Here ya go. Huh huh huh.

The crowd CHEERS.

ON ANDERSON'S CAMPER.

Tom is handcuffed roughly.

> **TOM**
> Now wait just a minute...

An agent comes out of the camper with a picture of Dallas. Bork grabs it and shows it to Tom.

> **BORK**
> How do you explain this?!

Flemming approaches Tom.

> **FLEMMING**
> Sooo, using two innocent teenagers as
> pawns in your sick game, huh?

> **TOM**
> I don't know what the hell...

> **FLEMMING**
> (disgusted)
> Take him away.

Anderson is dragged away past a group of young, boy-scout types who shake their heads in shame.

ANGLE ON Beavis and Butt-Head being interviewed by a reporter. Beavis is in his underwear. Tom is being dragged away in the background.

> **BEAVIS**
> I always thought there was something wrong
> with him. Heh heh heh.

> **BUTT-HEAD**
> Yeah, he had a lot of problems. Huh huh
> huh.

> **BEAVIS**
> Yeah, and um, he used to hit me too.

                    BUTT-HEAD
               (leaning towards camera)
        Uh hey, does anyone wanna see *my* unit?

                       B&B
        Huh huh huh huh huh huh.

DISSOLVE TO:

EXT.   WHITE HOUSE - DAY

Later. Establish. Most A.T.F. cars are pulling out.

INT.   WHITE HOUSE/OVAL OFFICE - DAY

B&B sit as Flemming paces in front of them. Beavis is no longer
Cornholio.

                       FLEMMING
               I gotta admit, I didn't believe it. I
               thought you were scum. But you saved more
               lives today than you'll ever know. You led
               us to one of the sickest criminals in our
               history. This country owes you a debt.

                       BUTT-HEAD
               Uh, does that mean, like, we're gonna get
               money and stuff?

                       BEAVIS
               Yeah, and chicks! We were supposed to
               score.

                       FLEMMING
               For security reasons, your actions will
               have to remain top secret. But someone
               very special wants to give his thanks.

Flemming motions to the big chair. The PRESIDENT swivels around and
rises to shake hands with B&B.

                       PRESIDENT
               Beavis and Butt-Head. On behalf of all
               your fellow Americans, I extend my deepest
               thanks. You exemplify a fine new crop of
               young Americans who will grow into the
               leaders of this great country.

                       BUTT-HEAD
               Huh huh huh. He said crap. Huh huh.

                       BEAVIS
               Heh heh. This guy's cool.

> **PRESIDENT**
> In recognition for your great service, I'm
> appointing you honorary agents in the
> Bureau of Alcohol, Tobacco and Firearms.

> **BUTT-HEAD**
> Whoa, huh huh!!!!

The President hands them citations.

> **BUTT-HEAD** (CONT.)
> You hear that, Beavis! We're gonna get
> alcohol, tobacco and guns!

> **BEAVIS**
> Yeah, maybe some chicks too. Heh heh.

B&B leave the office, muttering.

> **BUTT-HEAD**
> Cigarettes and beer rule! Huh huh.

> **BEAVIS**
> Yeah! We're with the bureau of cigarettes
> and chicks! We're gonna score!

> **B&B**
> Huh huh huh huh huh.

EXT.   AIRPORT NEAR B&B'S HOMETOWN - DAY

A plane lands.

INT.   PLANE/DOOR - DAY

As before, the flight crew stares in horror and silence as B&B deplane.

> **BUTT-HEAD**
> Uh... bye-bye.

> **BEAVIS**
> Heh heh. Bye bye. Heh heh.

EXT.   ELITE MOTEL LODGE BAR - DAY

Walking home, B&B pass the motel. They notice the sign for big screen
TV. They stop and look at it.

> **BUTT-HEAD**
> You know what else sucks? We never even
> got a TV.

ON BEAVIS, seeing something, amazed, ecstatic.

                    BEAVIS
          Heh mmm, heh mmm Butt-Head! Look!

Heavenly MUSIC. B&B stare at the wonder before them:

ANGLE ON THEIR TV, mangled, partly-crushed junk.

                    B&B
          Yes! Yes! Yes! Huh huh huh.

B&B run up to the set like it was their lost and found dog.

EXT.   RESIDENTIAL STREET - DAY

B&B walk off into the distance with the TV.

                    BEAVIS
          Hey Butt-Head, do you think we're ever
          gonna score?

                    BUTT-HEAD
          Uh, I probably will, but not you. You're
          too much of a butt-monkey. Huh huh.

                    BEAVIS
          Shut up, dill-hole.

                    BUTT-HEAD
          Butt-dumpling...

                    BEAVIS
          Turd-burglar...

                    BUTT-HEAD
          Dill-wad...

                    BEAVIS
          Bunghole...

                    BUTT-HEAD
          Butt-snatch...

                    BEAVIS
          Um, uh, butt... um, hole. Butt-hole...

                    BUTT-HEAD
          Uh... dill, um, face...

                    BEAVIS
          Um... ass... head...

BUTT-HEAD

Uh... butt-snatch...

BEAVIS

You already said that, Butt-Head.

BUTT-HEAD

Oh, uh, I mean, uh, ass-goblin...

B & B

Huh huh huh...

B&B head off into the sunset, trading lame insults as we **FADE OUT.**

END

STORYBOARD ART
AND
PUBLICITY STILLS

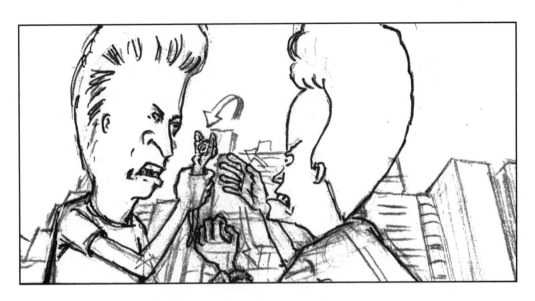

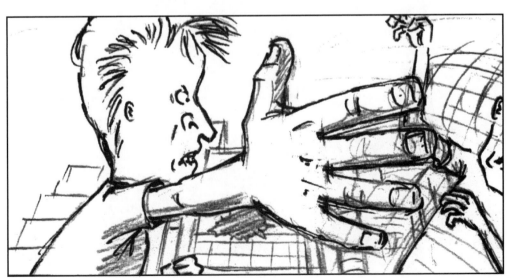

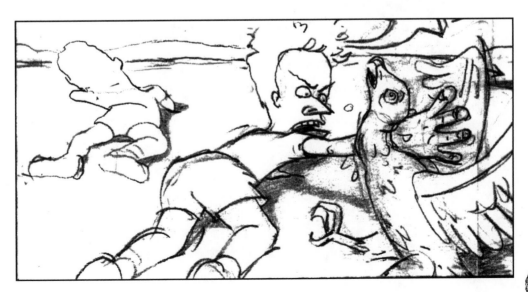

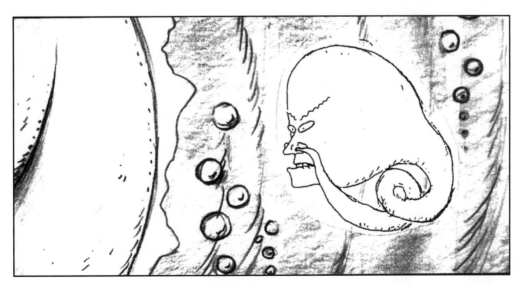